HEALTH,
LEADERSHIP
AND
ORGANISATIONS

Beyond The Shadow Side

Anna Eliatamby
(Editor)

ISBN: 978-1-912680-69-6 (paperback)

British Library Cataloguing in Publication Data.
A catalogue record for this book is available from the British Library.

Dedication

We dedicate this book to Ambassador William Lacey Swing, one of the greatest humanitarians and a holistic leader, whose heart was at the centre of his efforts. Some of us were lucky enough to have worked with him during his tenure as Director General of IOM (UN Migration Agency).

In very quiet ways, he led the organisation for ten years, saw it expand and, in 2016, formally join the United Nations. He was an inspiration to all of us who had the honour to work with him. He cared deeply for his staff and those IOM served. Every picture taken of him with the people IOM served naturally showed his profound humanity and humility.

He was an exemplar of true golden leadership and an inspiration to all. The memory of having worked with him remains.

Contributors

The production of this book has been a collective effort with many discussions and sharing of ideas. We hope that you will find our perspectives helpful and useful.

Don Braisby, Artist (Photographs), Ireland

Kerri Bridgewater, Consultant, South Africa

David Bryan, CBE, UK

Ransirini de Silva, Clinical Psychologist, Sri Lanka

Anna Eliatamby, Clinical Psychologist, UK

Michael Emery, Director, Human Resources, IOM (UN Migration Agency), Switzerland

Grazia Lomonte, Clinical Psychologist, Costa Rica

Marcus McDonald, Graphic Designer (Diagrams), UK

Greg Parston, Chair, Dartington Trust, UK

Robin Phillips and colleagues, Author Help

Jamie Ripman, Co-founder and Director, Practive, UK

Emmicki Roos, Expert, Women, Peace and Security Agenda at the Folke Bernadotte Academy (FBA), Sweden

Johan Schaar, Associate Senior Fellow with the Stockholm International Peace Research Institute (SIPRI), Chair, Active Learning Network for Accountability and Performance in Humanitarian Action (ALNAP), Sweden

Sonia Watson, OBE, Hon. FRIBA, Hon. FRIAS, Chief Executive of Blueprint for All, UK

Foreword

- -

What is the motivation for this book?

'Growth is not a battle to be hurried, but a slow walk down the road from home.'
—*Rithihi*

All of us, as leaders, often do our very best to be positive in our various roles and use golden behaviours to fulfil our functions. Similarly, most organisations will try to be ethical and value-based in how they function, what they expect from employees, and the cultures they create and maintain.

Most interventions in leadership, organisational change, and development also focus on building and enhancing the positive. These include leadership programmes, well-being initiatives, training, etc. And some of these are effective.

However, what we should acknowledge is that, alongside the golden, lies the shadow side of ourselves and organisations. All of us, regardless of how ethical and value-based we are, have shadow behaviours we use, hopefully, rarely. Similarly, organisational roles, cultures, and structures can possess shadow elements.

The core of unhealthy shadow aspects is sometimes known, or recognised but is usually not named, acknowledged, or addressed. Typically, we skirt around the concerns. A common intervention is to move the person who bullies or harasses to a new location rather than working with them to help them address the shadow and negative. A policy for dealing with inappropriate actions may be recognised as ineffective but steps to rectify this may not be taken.

The lack of acknowledgement has often led to some interventions to enhance positivity having a very limited impact or being torpedoed by the underlying shadow elements in either leaders or organisations. These shadow actions are also the ones that can have a significant and detrimental impact on overall health and deter the work of the organisation. Using these behaviours takes up energy and people's time that could be utilised in a much healthier way.

We suggest that, for leaders and organisations to operate healthily, we need to look at both aspects—the golden and shadow sides—and think about how we can enhance the positive and golden while addressing the shadow side and incorporating it, so it does not overwhelm the leader in their role or the organisation in its function.

Our book offers you two models, one for leaders and the other for organisations, to explore the golden and shadow aspects and how they are part of us as individual leaders and as organisations. First, we begin with a description of our models and explain the separate parts of them with many examples—both positive and negative. Second, we provide you with a description of the shadow behaviours and the golden ones (giving respect, being compassionate) and attempt to understand them from a psychological standpoint.

Finally, we provide you with some exercises and suggestions for you (individually or collectively) to explore your own identity/role as a leader or organisation and bring about change to address the shadow and negative while enhancing and building the positive. We also have a chapter of expert voices for us all to learn from their experience.

Throughout the book, we use quotes or stories from individuals or fictitious ones. Where possible, we have provided you with names, e.g. Anna refers to Anna Eliatamby.

It is time for all of us to do what we commonly fail to do, as we are fallible human beings who rarely stop and reflect. To explore so that we can grow as individuals, as organisations and become more wholesome so our contribution to the world is healing and long lasting. We deserve it for ourselves and for those who will lead the world after we have finished our work.

This book has been separated into three sections as you will see. There is a photograph at the end of each section so that you can pause and reflect on what you have just read.

You may prefer to focus on one section or read each one in turn. Of course, the choice is yours.

Please take your time and contact us if you have any questions.

Thank you.

www.healthyleadership.world

Contents

SECTION THREE
Where Next?

Section One

Our Approach

Chapter One

Our Rationale And The Models For Healthy
Leadership And Organisations

Our rationale

We have each worked in many types of organisations, from tiny, family-run entities to large global ones in various sectors—private, public, and not-for-profit. There is a common thread to these experiences: traditionally, they have wonderful people who use golden behaviours alongside those using negative ones such as bullying and harassment, and perhaps fraud or corruption (shadow). Would you agree?

Both facets exist in individuals and organisations, often side by side. The golden is sometimes acknowledged, but the shadow is rarely acknowledged or tackled. For example, low level lying and hypocrisy are often known about but rarely truly addressed.

Why does this happen? Where can we find answers to this dilemma? Perhaps in the field of leadership? Having been involved in this sector and reflecting on the many models and interventions, we realise that they only offer part of the answer. Concepts, such as transformational versus transactional, collective leadership, and interventions (leadership programmes) help by giving us theoretical frameworks and skills-oriented interventions that often only touch the surface of the issue. Reading about leadership or being sent on a programme may give the person some ideas on how to behave, but there is often no guarantee that they will change their work actions and approaches. Understanding these concepts does not really help us comprehend why the golden and shadow aspects often co-exist in individuals and organisations.

(The only leadership programme that some of us know does work is one that focuses on the behaviours of the person through sessions with an expert in acting and coaching. Very few interventions look at the seamier side of individuals and organisations. Laura Crawshaw is so successful in addressing negative behaviours that she is known as the Boss Whisperer.)

Some have adopted Jung's terms of golden and shadow sides as an explanatory concept, e.g. Gerard Egan. These concepts make sense as a framework for understanding. (It is interesting to note that much of what Jung and others describe as golden and shadow are found in early writings of Buddhism.) Golden and shadow aspects can apply to the individual and the group. This concept is a central tenet of this book's approach.

The golden side refers to those very positive thoughts, emotions, and behaviours we can have and use, e.g. kindness, honesty, and integrity. The shadow side comprises all the negative aspects of human beings' thoughts, emotions, and behaviours such as rudeness, aggression, slyness, and criminality. Each varies in terms of severity and impact on the recipient(s).

Carl Jung and Robert Johnson (Jungian psychoanalyst) emphasise the importance of looking at both and the fact that they are often reflected in each other. What is golden (e.g. being diplomatic) can have its counterpart in the shadow (e.g. a desire, when you are running low on patience, to tell someone what you think of them when in a very sensitive meeting).

Often, we can be aware of and choose to work from the golden aspects of ourselves or from the shadow sides. We can endeavour to be polite and professional in our work, however there may be times when we flip over to the shadow side and, for example, are rude to someone. In these circumstances, we will usually realise what we have done, return to the golden side, and apologise.

We suggest that there is a continuum from golden to shadow and vice versa and, sometimes, it is difficult to recognise whether a thought or behaviour or action is golden or shadow. For example, giving someone a present as a thank you but offering them something that you don't want. Deciding if something is golden or shadow or in-between will depend on the interpreter of these actions or thoughts.

In this book, we provide models based on the concepts of golden and shadow, for individuals and organisations, so that we can really explore why individuals and organisations rarely tackle the negative shadow side in a way that is healing and helpful to all. The models allow us to properly attend to both simultaneously. We will not be delving into why these phenomena exist, as that discussion is one where we cannot generate an answer in this lifetime. It is, for us, simpler to assume that they exist, examine and then use them to understand ourselves as individuals and members of organisations.

The aim of the models is to provide us with a sensible, holistic way of conceptualising individuals and organisations. Using this as the focus of this book, we can look at, in depth, how to enhance the positive and heal and tackle the negative in individuals and organisations. Key premises are that healing starts with an acknowledgement of what is in the past and present (helpful and negative), understanding these factors and then learning how to mend, recognising that it is a continuous, lifelong process.

The model does not explain the neuroscience of human beings; it is merely a way for us to think about how humans operate, heal, or harm. Neuroscience, like the study of psychology, has investigated different human functions separately. There is now talk of interconnections such as between emotions and cognitions, but this research is at an early stage. It is easy to see why functions are being studied separately because of the enormity of the task, but this does not help an individual holistically understand how they work. This book is an attempt to synthesise how we function, at least at the conceptual level.

The key elements of the models

What is overall healthiness?

The words healthy and healthiness usually refer to physical health and, sometimes, mental health and well-being. All these facets are important components for overall healthiness, but we suggest that there are others that also must be taken into consideration. These include the degree of synergy between purpose, values, and how life is lived and work conducted; the impact of material resources and the environment; being willing to be open and listen to the incoming future and finally how we live and cope with the shadow side.

All these factors, for overall healthiness, need to be coordinated with compassion and respect by our individual or organisational sense of Self.

What is healthy leadership?

Leadership is an individual and collective function that has many intentions. This usually includes an aim to serve human beings and/or something. For some, leadership is operationalised ethically and positively to serve others. Others will have another focus, such as a profit motive alongside wanting to be ethical.

Healthy leadership happens when the individual or the group do their utmost to serve others ethically and respectfully, while acknowledging that there can be negativity and being willing to address it and heal. They remain flexible and open to sensing the incoming future.

What is a healthy organisation?

Why do organisations exist? Usually, to enact a greater purpose which can be forgotten as the organisation becomes bigger and veers from the intended path.

A healthy organisation ensures it remains true to its purpose, and that is to do no harm to humans or the planet. Do no harm. The organisation always endeavours to provide a nourishing culture and structure within which people can grow and flourish in their work to achieve the purpose. A healthy organisation works to recognise and address unhealthy elements, is amenable to change and is willing to consider possible futures while operating in the present.

Here are two diagrams depicting our models: the individual and the organisation.

The diagrams contain only dotted lines on purpose, as every aspect is porous and inter-connects with all the other facets in the diagram. All the components in both diagrams will contribute to the overall healthiness of individuals and organisations, beyond well-being, mental health, and physical health.

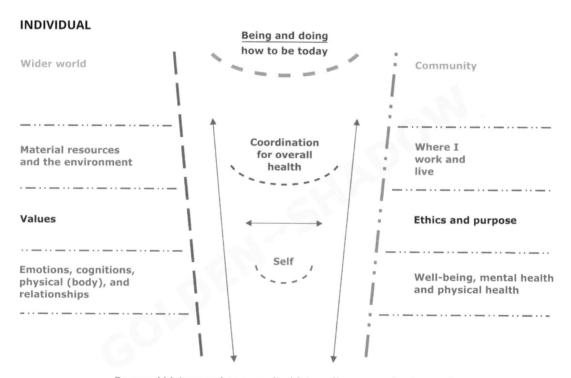

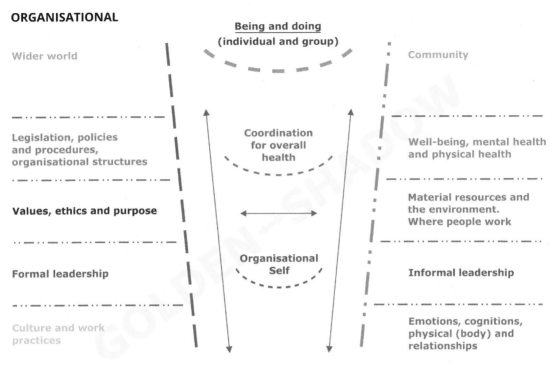

ORGANISATIONAL

Wider world

Being and doing
(individual and group)

Community

Legislation, policies
and procedures,
organisational structures

Coordination
for overall
health

Well-being, mental health
and physical health

Values, ethics and purpose

Material resources and
the environment.
Where people work

Formal leadership

Organisational
Self

Informal leadership

Culture and work
practices

Emotions, cognitions,
physical (body) and
relationships

Organisational history (known and unknown)

GOLDEN–SHADOW

Golden, shadow and consciousness

We adopt the concept of golden and shadow (as described above). This often overlaps with what is conscious and unconscious. For both, golden and shadow, there are behaviours, emotions, and thoughts that we are aware of and then some aspects of which we are completely unaware that sometimes come to the surface. We suggest that there is a continuum from golden to shadow and that they are inter-related (the latter suggested by Jung and others). We also propose that there is a balance between golden and shadow, sometimes for positivity and, occasionally, for negativity (shadow). Interpreting what is golden and what is shadow will vary and depend on the person (or people) judging the behaviours, thoughts, and emotions, and the overall situation.

Golden behaviours (and accompanying thoughts and emotions) include honesty, being ethical, kindness, generosity, respect, compassion, diplomacy, politeness, inclusion, and respect for diversity. Shadow behaviours and thoughts and emotions are mainly the diametrical opposite of golden behaviours: dishonesty, immorality, disrespect, bullying, harassment, being inconsiderate, and disrespect for difference and diversity. Shadow behaviours can infringe an organisation's policies and procedures and, at times, are illegal.

As mentioned above, for us, there is a continuum from shadow to golden. What is golden can have its counterpart in shadow. It is also important to know that these are not two distinct sets but are inter-related and we all possess both shadow and golden behaviours, thoughts, and emotions. Anna did a self-analysis of her golden and shadow behaviours and tried to categorise them. She realised that the intention behind a behaviour was often what defined it as golden or not. Some of these behaviours are in our conscious realm and others are not.

Each behaviour, thought, and emotion (golden or shadow) has a purpose and function in our lives and can be triggered and maintained by different aspects of our lives. They are interconnected with all the elements (as shown in the diagram) and will manifest in those elements in different ways. Part of the journey is to explore the purpose and function of all these behaviours, thoughts, and emotions.

Does consciousness exist? We have investigated this issue by considering what Jung, Freud and others have said, including neuroscientists such as Anil Seth, Antonio Damasio, and Mark Solms. Some say that consciousness exists, but there is much debate about its nature, function, and location. We will not be looking into any of these questions but will simply assume that it exists, alongside the unconscious, and is linked to the golden and shadow. (The Royal Institute of Great Britain has some excellent videos on YouTube of talks by these neuroscientists and others.) Others, in the field of therapy, acknowledge the presence of the unconscious and explore it, both theoretically and practically.

Organisations also have conscious and unconscious aspects. These can be golden or shadow with associated behaviours, thoughts, and emotions. How these came into being is interesting. Often it is the individuals, at its inception, who define the organisation, and leaders and employees who come along later then refine it. A good way of understanding the conscious and unconscious aspects of an organisation is by looking at its artefacts such as decoration, office size, and whether there are groups of employees who determine, positively or negatively, what is acceptable in terms of behaviour and culture.

The Self as a repository

Another concept we would like to include is that of the Self (individual and group). (We capitalise the word self to demarcate when we are referring to the individual or group Self). Once again, much has been written about what is Self and where we can find it from a neuroscience perspective. This issue is probably not going to be resolved soon. We adopt the view that it is the coordinating part of ourselves across the whole of our individual neuroscience. Perhaps we can also assume the same for group Self, although the research is less clear.

Having looked at the work of neuroscience and psychology, it makes sense to have a place (the Self) that defines who I am as well as coordinating all our different components as in the models to ensure overall health. The Self is also fluid and, while having a central core, can be affected by any of the other components as described in the diagram.

From a neuroscience perspective, research is showing that there is much more flexibility and plasticity in how our neural systems function, and they are influenced by how we behave and interact with the wider world. For example, research has shown that acting/role playing can have a positive influence on our neural systems and subsequent emotions and behaviour (Thorpe, 2019).

The Organisational Self can also be a coordinator, but this is likely heavily influenced by those deemed to be leaders. If the leader is charismatic, purpose-focussed, and democratic, then the Organisational Self is likely to be positive and reflect the leader's characteristics. If a leader really cares for staff, remembers people's names, and greets them, then others in the organisation are likely to feel that they should also work to be more respectful. People will also readily make that extra effort to achieve the purpose of the organisation and work on the golden side.

The sense of Self, collectively, can also be shadow. There was an influential organisation that viewed itself as value based and expected its employees to reflect this. However, one of the senior people had a reputation for bullying and this was never tackled, even when staff went to the Chief Executive asking for help. It was brushed off as their problem. Other employees recognised this and behaved unscrupulously, e.g. excluding colleagues, and stealing other people's work and ideas.

If a person's sense of Self is healthy and positive, then they are more likely to stay on the golden side and choose positive behaviours using their values as a guide, even if the prevailing Organisational Self is shadow. Not that they won't have negative thoughts, emotions, and behaviours, e.g. jealousy, but they are less likely to let the shadow side heavily influence them. If, however, someone's Self is negative, then they are likely to choose those behaviours that reinforce the shadow in the same circumstances.

An individual's sense of Self will often determine how they enact their assigned role and therefore which behaviours they will use, golden or shadow. Similarly, an organisational sense of Self may influence the roles and assigned behaviours of leadership and other positions.

We also suggest that it is through the Self that, if we permit ourselves, we can sense the future. Otto Scharmer's model has many useful descriptions on how we can do this. We have incorporated this perspective here.

Self and overall health (well-being, mental health and physical health)

As mentioned above, the Self has a coordinating function, and it is also the place where a sense of overall health occurs. In this model, overall health is an outcome and linked to other aspects of the person. It can be positive or negative and will influence the person both in the short or long term. The sources for overall health include the extent to which there is a synergy between the person's values and purpose and how they are living and working.

Assuming positive values and purpose are used, then overall healthiness is likely to be high if there is great congruence between them and the person's lifestyle. If there are low levels of equivalence, then a person's sense of overall healthiness will probably be negative. The extent to which the person is compassionate and considerate of others is also a vital potential source of overall health. These are very important factors identified by the Dalai Lama and B. Allan Wallace.

Another source of overall healthiness is the person's well-being, mental health and physical health, and the extent to which they are looking after themselves. The last source is their physical environment and related factors, such as material goods and money and the pursuit of sustainability. Collectively, all these factors contribute to a person's overall healthiness and can affect how they function in the world.

At the organisational level, coordination and overall healthiness are also essential and seen as being steered by the collective Self. Commonly, the sense of Self and associated coordination is guided by an often un-elected group of individuals who carry a lot of informal power and authority.

Well-being programmes in organisations are often interventions which can be valuable and include access to counselling and education on stress management and resilience. While these are usually effective, they rarely address the need for synergy with purpose and ethics, mental and physical health, the physical and material world, and compassion and respect. All these need to be considered at the organisational level for there to be holistic, positive overall healthiness in the organisation.

Emotions, cognitions, physical (body), and relationships

As human beings, we comprise emotions, cognitions (thinking, attention, decision-making, memories) and the physical (our bodies). More and more is being learned about how these functions work and how they inter-relate. This is an exciting time in neuroscience and psychology as researchers explore the function and location of each of these.

The study of the role of emotions has developed since some of us were undergraduates in the 1970s. They have key functions in our lives: influencing attention, motivating behaviours, and determining the significance of what happens. These occur at the level of the individual, between individuals, and there is also a social and cultural function.

We are social animals belonging to families and communities in our own individual and collective ways. Some of us are very gregarious and have a large inner and outer social network, and others are content with a smaller circle of support. These issues apply at home and work.

Research in this field is working on identifying the interplay between emotions and cognitions. There is much debate about which parts of the brain, including neural networks, are responsible for emotions.

Traditionally, the knowledge and skills we have gained reside in our memory system. Memory is where we encode information we receive, store, and then retrieve as needed. We possess different types of memory: sensory memory (fleeting) and short term and long term. Long-term memory includes episodic memory (events that happened) and semantic (general knowledge).

Memories of traumatic or difficult events are often encoded differently to other memories and have an extra emotional loading that can negatively affect the person. This can lead to problems in the present if there has not been a sufficient resolution of the past trauma or difficulty.

Our physical bodies are involved in the expression of emotions and behaviours. The senses received from the body impact our brains and emotions in many ways through interoception. Additionally, people can have body memories, especially of traumatic events, and stimuli can trigger these in the present if the person has not sufficiently resolved psychological factors linked to the traumatic memory.

Organisations possess some of these qualities, such as memories, what is acceptable as emotional behaviour, etc. In any establishment, there will be those who are the keepers of memories, and they are, sometimes, not acknowledged.

The wider world and community

We influence the world, and it affects us. We may not always recognise this, but it is a daily occurrence. The largest example to date is the COVID-19 pandemic. It made us all re-think our frames for how we lived and worked. We went into a period of shock, from which we are still emerging, and learned how to live smaller lives. The high levels of stress and anxiety had an impact and, for some, there was a greater tendency to be negative and use harmful coping mechanisms and behaviours. For example, somehow, having to live in a high-risk zone with rules imposed by others made some individuals use high-risk negative behaviours, such as disappearing for a weekend because they wanted freedom. Not sensible at all. Globally, we had examples of people carrying out high-risk actions in the middle of the pandemic, such as hosting parties for large groups or refusing to wear masks. These behaviours will, hopefully, decrease with time.

For most of us, even in COVID times, we engage positively in our external world and communities and will occasionally stop and think about how they influence us. We remain open to learning from the world and contributing to it. The BBC reported that Mr Rohit Suri, a landlord in Delhi (India), made sure that a meal was ready for his tenant, Dr Kaushik Barua, when he returned home from being on duty in a critical care ward. Similarly, police officers in Panchkula took time to give a birthday cake and sing Happy Birthday to Mr Puri, who was an older person living alone.

Organisations are influenced by what is going on in the world around them. An obvious example is the impact of the #MeToo and #BlackLivesMatter movements. Almost everybody in an organisation will have known (tacitly or unconsciously) that discrimination and associated behaviours existed in their corporations, but most did little beyond creating policies and offering awareness training. Diverse people often felt that they could not speak up. These movements have and are continuing to uncover, sometimes through the courage of individuals, the fault lines in business and society.

For some entities, suddenly, there are many *mea culpa* public statements and actions. A recent one was the appointment and then resignation of Alexi McCammond, Teen Vogue Editor. It had been discovered that she had written and then deleted racist tweets about Asians as well as homophobic utterances in her younger days. What is curious is that very senior people in Condé Nast had considered some tweets and their potential impact but had still offered her the post. The public indignation and concern of Teen Vogue staff and others led to her resignation even though she had publicly apologised. Some argue that this is part of the woke culture. It is important to remember that, even though these comments were made over ten years ago, they perhaps speak to a pattern of thought. What is the evidence, apart from a public apology, that she has learned from her past? Hopefully, there has been some as she has been re-employed by Axios.

Culture and work practices

The culture of an organisation has many factors that influence it, some of which are described above and below. Fons Trompenaars describes the key elements - basic assumptions and norms and values which are then linked/demonstrated by the artefacts and products such as work practices.

The social rules of what is acceptable are often unwritten and developed by those who are no longer present. A very simple indicator of this is seen to be what is suitable in terms of clothing. The technology and ways of working in an organisation are often idiosyncratic, will have historical reasons for their existence, and will vary from organisation to organisation, e.g. which computing equipment is preferred.

Formal and informal leadership

We have observed that formal and informal leadership exists in almost all organisations. The formal leaders are the ones with the job title and the informal people may not have the position but can certainly hold power. In healthy organisations, both parties acknowledge each other's existence and work together. In unhealthy organisations, they can be confrontational and, sometimes, it is the informal leaders who are dominant.

Legislation, policies and procedures, organisational structures

These are vital components of an organisation. The elegant ones are often simple, easy to understand and implement. The more complex they are, the less chance that people will remember or use them.

A crucial factor is the extent to which they are understood and operationalised. This can be done in a positive way or used punitively to gain control. For example, a manager, knowing that contract renewal is dependent on a good assessment of past work, may threaten staff with this.

Material resources and the environment (including where we work)

How we are, as individual leaders and organisations, is also influenced by the pursuit for sustainability. The climate crisis is something that we know about, but we rarely see its impact on our lives, and this is important as it affects us both in the short and long term.

We are also influenced by the material resources available to us in our personal and work lives. This includes where we work; these environments can be conducive or the opposite.

Values, purpose, and ethics

All of us as individuals and members of establishments will, if asked, be able to articulate our values and ethics and, perhaps, our sense of purpose. These three often provide meaning in our lives. Some of us will have badges and clothing to match. Businesses often use their purpose and value statements as part of their branding and advertising.

The test is whether we operationalise these in real life. The values of the current English National Health Service (NHS) are very similar to those in 1945 when it was launched, including some of the wording. Very interesting branding. However, when you look at the current organisational structure and intentions, you see that much of the NHS is now run by private sector entities and it exists as a public body only in name. This was not what Aneurin (Nye) Bevan and William Beveridge envisaged when they conceived of a free national health service. However, people in charge of the NHS today are likely to argue that it is still a public body.

At the individual level, there are those who will tell you they are ethical, but when you review their past and current actions, there is powerful evidence to the contrary. Someone could continue to profess that they have stolen nothing from the organisation, even when there is paperwork showing bank transfers from corporate accounts into their own personal ones. Others (individually and organisationally) will, 99 percent of the time, be ethical and purpose driven with only a minor blip, which they often put right.

The same applies to organisations. This includes the humanitarian sector where you would expect greater adherence to purpose, to serve others. Some, regardless of sector, will be honourable in working towards purpose, and others will not.

Purpose is a vital component for each of us. Okinawa, Japan, is one place that has a significant number of older people over 90 years. Dr Suzuki identified the factors that contributed, including *ikigai* (having a personal mission) such as remaining interested in helping the community and wanting to support grandchildren.

Having a sense of purpose or duty is key to how we are as individuals or members of an organisation. It is our moral code. It interacts with our sense of Self, and this will steer us towards being golden or can shift us to the shadow side if we ignore our sense of purpose.

Hatami and Hilton Segel (2021) noted that organisations where there is a clear sense of purpose outperform those without. Employees who state that they can live their purpose at work are also better and more loyal staff.

Our past and its influence on our present

What happened to us as we grew up, who was in our lives as well as where and how we lived, shaped us. Most of us had positive experiences, carers, and supporters in our lives and these influenced us to be positive also and on the golden side of life. Anna's father allowed his children to grow up freely and make their own decisions, and he enabled them to have a very good schooling. He said, 'The best thing you can leave your child is an excellent education.'

Of course, there were negative encounters and people, e.g. the classmate at school who felt it necessary to whisper, in Anna's presence, that she smelled, and they affected some of her school life. Being bullied by a friend was another negative experience. These influenced and shaped Anna's shadow side.

Some of the earlier experiences will also have an influence on our daily lives. Anna often encourages younger colleagues to seek further education (remembering her father's words). She is sometimes, initially, intimidated by people who bear a resemblance to the friend who bullied her until she remembers that she is older and knows how to tackle such behaviour.

Our past explains who we are but does not have to shape our current selves and behaviours.

In Anna's clinical work, she has worked with some people who had awful experiences but chose to take a different approach. 'My managers were domineering and insensitive (like my father used to be). Now that I am one, I will not do that.'

Some, unfortunately, for some reason best known to themselves, will persistently take the shadow path. Often, those who display negative behaviours have experienced similar actions in their past. Tacitly, the child or younger person may normalise these behaviours as acceptable.

Some have developed the ability to suppress, perhaps because of their history. This tendency can be a benefit, especially in the humanitarian sector, when you sometimes must deal with the unspeakable sides of humanity. However, this inclination can also help someone carry out very negative behaviours towards another colleague. The perpetrator may not give themselves permission to think of the emotional consequences for themselves or the targeted person.

There is a view that the business world includes those who have sociopathic or psychopathic tendencies. Assuming this to be the case, these individuals are more likely to be inclined to use shadow behaviours. It is doubtful that they will see that using these as problematic and often have a good rationale for their continued use. Individuals who show these behaviours and who use forensic services have often had traumatic backgrounds. It is not clear if this is also the case for individuals with similar behaviours and who are in business.

The past of an organisation can also influence the present. It is almost like the flavour of the past (golden and shadow) permeates the present, partly by those who have been with the organisation for a long time and in other ways that we have yet to understand.

There was an organisation (not for profit) that had, for many years, a positive culture and behaviours were on the golden side, i.e. ethical and people oriented. However, in a particular part of the system, it was known that staff could be promoted by paying for it, sometimes through money or having sex with senior leaders. This knowledge gave permission for others, lower down, to behave also unscrupulously, i.e. the shadow side prevailed. Interestingly, later, when the leadership changed and more scrupulous people led that section, the whole flavour and culture changed to the golden side. We will explore this further on.

Interactions

These are not simple models at all, and some would describe them as messy, which is true. But so are human beings and organisations. The models are conceptual, based on experience and what we know of research. Hopefully, they are helpful.

All the components of each model interact and flow within and between each other. Hence the dotted lines.

The coordinator is the individual Self or the Organisational Self, which draws from the other facets and influences them. This is very much an assumption on our part and is a conceptual suggestion and recommendation to make sense of why we sometimes are wholesome and golden and then hurtful and shadow at other times.

When there is harmony and flow across our sense of Self, then we are likely to operate from the golden side of ourselves as opposed to the shadow side. The Self helps us to maintain balance and homeostasis and will aid us to have positive outcomes in terms of overall health.

The models represent the backbone of this book, and we will use them throughout to explain behaviours and assessments. We will use the models to adopt a different approach in terms of individual and organisational interventions.

Chapter Two

Golden And Shadow Behaviours, Thoughts, And Emotions

There are so many behaviours (and associated thoughts) and emotions that we could consider here, and they are easy to list. We will only focus on the most common ones and on the psychology underpinning them so we can have a greater understanding of people who use these behaviours.

We found this chapter a little difficult to write because of some topics. It can also be hard to read about these, be they golden or shadow, partly because we rarely stop and consider ourselves meaningfully. It can be helpful, as we did when writing, to pause and return when ready.

We suggest that, before you start this chapter, you halt and think about two key events in your history (individual and organisational) that have had an impact, and which you remember. They can be positive or negative in terms of outcome. For both events, what was your role and what were the golden and shadow behaviours, thoughts, and emotions shown by you? Please consider your reflections and write as many of your golden and shadow behaviours, thoughts, and emotions as you can recall. Thank you.

Golden behaviours, thoughts, and emotions

These include kindness, compassion, being positive, and being respectful. There are, of course, many more, but we would like to include these as they, to us, are the bedrock for decency as an individual and for organisations.

Self-esteem

Verywellmind.com describes this term as a 'person's overall subjective sense of personal worth or value'. It is also used inter-changeably with self-confidence, self-worth, and self-regard.

Several factors, including status, health, and age can have an impact on self-esteem and how you think about yourself. It can affect many aspects of life, such as decision-making, well-being and mental health, motivation, and relationships. Issues in the living environment can also positively or adversely affect a person's self-esteem, e.g. discrimination, constant criticism, or praise.

Those with high levels of self-esteem understand well their capabilities and skills, have lofty expectations of themselves, and can develop and keep healthy relationships. They can communicate effectively. Indicators of a positive level of self-esteem are trust and belief in yourself, considering that you are equal to others, being good at communication, expressing needs, and getting and maintaining relationships. The person will also be appropriately assertive, realistic, accepting about themselves, and will tend not to dwell on the past.

However, people who are overly confident are likely to overestimate their strengths and feel entitled, with little justification. Such individuals can find it hard to acquire and keep good relationships. They can also be narcissistic.

Conversely, people with low levels of self-esteem are less confident in themselves and their capabilities and are likely to doubt themselves, e.g. not feel worthy. They could believe that they are not equal to others, focus on their weaknesses, experience a lot of self-doubt, lack confidence, and find it hard to accept positive feedback. If the person persistently has very low self-esteem, then they could be at risk for anxiety or depression.

Research shows that the precursors for an adult's self-esteem lie in their upbringing, mainly parenting styles. A positive and enhancing parental approach will build positive and realistic self-esteem. A negative and critical parental approach can lead to low levels of self-esteem, especially if school, friends, and work colleagues then reinforce this. Occasionally, someone with low self-esteem may carry out an act that leads to reinforcement of their low levels, e.g. not meeting a deadline (even though it is possible) knowing that this will lead to criticism.

Experience shows that self-esteem is not a static characteristic, and it can fluctuate depending on the circumstance and your mood. It is worth thinking of perhaps carrying reminders to encourage you to regain your usual level of self-esteem, e.g. wearing a bracelet that reminds you to be confident.

You can build your self-esteem by considering how you think of yourself. What are your positive and negative thoughts? How can you replace the negative with more positive statements and how can you prompt yourself to be more positive? What can you do to enhance your self-care and compassion?

If you are working with someone who has low self-esteem, it is worth understanding the person and quietly and slowly help them build their self-confidence in a way that is comfortable for them. Conversely, if the person has exaggerated levels of self-esteem, then it is important to be assertive yet inclusive with them. Remember, the overly high levels of self-esteem may be a protection against feeling very insecure.

Compassion

Compassion refers to our empathy and concern for others, coupled with an authentic desire to help and act accordingly. It differs from empathy, which rarely leads to action.

Studies show that we are most likely to experience compassion when we perceive another's situation to be serious, unjust (not self-inflicted) and relatable to ourselves (eliciting empathy). Research by David Rand shows that adults' and children's first impulse is to help others. Compassion is seen as intrinsic and allows us to support each other in life.

Well-being, mental health, and physical health are usually enhanced if we are compassionate. A range of experiments have shown that the act of giving, whether it be our time, money, or skills, gives us pleasure. For example, a study by Dunn and Aknin (2008) showed a strong positive correlation between spending money on others (not yourself) and personal well-being, regardless of individual circumstances, e.g. income level, perceived freedom.

Compassion helps us to broaden our perspective to other people. This then augments our sense of connection to others. When we do something for someone else, we shift our focus outside the individual Self and increase our sense of connection to others. People who feel close connections to others are said to be more likely to trust others, cooperate, and have higher self-esteem. They also report lower levels of depression and anxiety. This encourages others to be more open to trust and cooperation. Compassionate behaviour, such as volunteer work, has been associated with positive outcomes, for instance, increased self-esteem among adolescents, and improved mortality rates among older volunteers. In contrast, low social connection is associated with declines in physical health and mental health.

By motivating us to help others, compassion gives us a sense of empowerment and agency—by taking action to relieve someone else's situation, we improve our own sense of resilience and well-being.

When we witness compassionate acts by others, we nurture our own sense of compassion. Research by Jonathan Haidt suggests that seeing a person being helped creates a state of 'elevation'—which inspires us to support others. Haidt showed that corporate leaders 'who engage in self-sacrificing behaviour' and elicit elevation in their employees, secure greater influence among their employees, who then act with more compassion in the workplace.

Dutton, Workman, and Harding (2014) studied compassion in the workplace and have identified six relevant organisational aspects:

- Shared values that an organisation and its people perceive to be important
- Shared organisational beliefs
- Shared organisational behaviours that are used by employees to interact with one another
- Organisational practices which support and shape compassion
- Structure and quality of relationships between employees
- Leaders' behaviours, specifically the signalling and modelling of appropriate behaviours and response to employees' situations and difficulties.

A compassionate workplace depends on the creation of an inclusive organisational culture, in which all employees commit to listen, and work to comprehend one another's diverse experiences, challenges and perspectives. It requires a commitment to recognise when people are struggling and, without judgement, work to support them and ease the problems they're experiencing. This approach helps employees feel connected and supported—improving their resilience, productivity, and commitment to the organisation. We should extend this compassionate approach to customers and clients. Leaders, managers and colleagues should commit to ensuring that employees and customers feel they are seen and heard.

Lonczak (2021) noted that a wide range of individuals and groups with power, from policymakers to the police, teachers, parents, doctors, nurses, and CEOs can positively influence societal issues such as home-lessness through the practice and use of compassion-oriented actions. Being compassionate at work significantly improves relationships and willingness to work together, as well as increasing the possibility of success.

She suggests we can teach ourselves to become more compassionate by being altruistic—engaging in acts of service to help people, animals, and communities, and avoiding judgement—we can't know exactly how and why someone has ended up in a particular situation, nor how we would have coped (given the same circumstances), so we should refrain from judging them and consider how similar we are to one another and practice gratitude. She also suggests that we need to be kind to ourselves—remembering that everyone is flawed and makes mistakes, and we serve ourselves and others best by forgiving our mistakes and moving forward positively.

Studies have shown that various compassion and meditation practices, usually derived from traditional Buddhist practices, may help cultivate compassion, increase feelings of closeness and connection, and promote altruistic feelings. (Participants were asked to imagine a time when someone was finding life difficult, and to wish for the relief of that person's situation. They were required to practise experiencing compassion for different people, from someone they would easily feel compassion for, such as a family member, to strangers and people with whom they have had difficulties or conflicts.)

Researchers have found that people who receive short-term compassion training experience greater empathy, or emotional understanding, of others and are more likely to engage in helpful, or pro-social, behaviours towards others. Studies have also shown compassionate meditation helps people become more satisfied themselves.

It is, of course, vital to develop and maintain a sense of compassion for Self. Without this, we are likely to find it very difficult to be more compassionate towards others and communities.

Kindness

What is it?

Peterson and Seligman (2004) define kindness as 'doing favours and good deeds for others; helping them; taking care of them.' While kindness can be about putting someone else's needs before our own, the two components of kindness are being kind (to others and self) and receiving kindness from others. Wisdom from cultures, across civilisations and time, recognises that humans need to practice kindness to thrive and be fully alive and these qualities are cornerstones for well-being, mental health and physical health.

Humans are social creatures who rely on communal connections to survive and thrive. Professor Dacher Keltner (2012) observes that humans need to be kind or use kindness towards each other to overcome social conflicts and create cohesion. Although some acts of kindness are related to social instincts, such as putting your arm in front of someone when the brakes hit or pushing someone back to save them from falling, learning to be kind is also possible.

Kindness helps you note the similarities in each other rather than the differences and can deepen solidarity in communities and unlock our shared humanity. Some say that humans have a built-in capacity to be cooperative, pro-social, and altruistic. We see this in young children who naturally support each other, expecting no external reinforcement—praise or reward. It then seems kindness has in-built or intrinsic rewards, making the act of kindness itself pleasurable or rewarding. External rewards should not be present for in-built pleasure to take effect. Further, children who exhibit kind behaviour connect well with others socially, are more accepted by peers, and are unlikely to engage in activities such as bullying.

In adulthood, we value kindness and search for it in family and when choosing life partners. A study conducted by Kniffin and Sloan Wilson (2004) observed that personal characteristics directly influence the perception of physical attractiveness. Kind people were rated higher in physical attractiveness. However, as humans grow and adapt to modern society, acts of kindness and collaboration are often discouraged and replaced with competition and the race for individual achievement.

Kindness and you

Positive psychology recognises kindness for its significance as a character strength and virtue. Kindness encompasses positivity, creates the opposite experience brought on by negative emotions, and facilitates acknowledging that we and others are worth caring for as equal living beings. It allows us to pay attention to the needs of others and provide meaning in taking actions on behalf of others. Kindness ultimately pushes us to behave better towards ourselves and others. The experience of giving and receiving it provides the opportunity for us to connect to others and our environment in a more profound and meaningful manner.

Regardless of where one stands on the continuum of mental health, ranging from mental illness to mental wellness, the use and practice of kindness encourages mental wellness. Kindness empowers you to feel happy, energised, engaged, and content with life. Simply put, being kind helps with feeling good and boosting your mood. Being kind comes easily for some but is a deliberate effort for others. Whichever mode kindness comes in, the mental health benefits of being kind are vast.

Why should we be kind to others?

'No act of kindness, however small, is ever wasted.'
—*Aesop*

Social psychology studies report that helping behaviour is contagious. When someone engages in a kind act, it benefits the recipient of the gesture and the person who is engaging in the action (and those who witness the act) and encourages others to be helpful.

The advantages of acts of kindness are both emotional and physiological. For example, a study conducted by Cutler and Campbell-Meiklejohn (2018) found that in brain scans of thousands of people who engaged in acts of kindness (regardless of whether it was strategic or altruistic), people experienced the feel-good 'warm glow' effect through the experience of a rush of endorphins. Observation of increased brain activity in specific regions, when the act of kindness was specifically altruistic with no expectations of gains in return, showed the unique physiological impact of kindness.

Additionally, physical benefits of the experience of kindness over time include increased lifespan, more energy, reduced pain, and lowered blood pressure. Psychological benefits include the occurrence of empathy, compassion, gratitude, and an increased sense of community. Further, mental health benefits can include reduced stress and anxiety, improved resilience, increased pleasure, reduced depression, and increased overall well-being.

Why should we be kind to ourselves?

The physiological and psychological reactions and benefits are also present for self-kindness. Although being kind to others can be common, most ignore kindness to themselves or are uncomfortable receiving kind gestures. Kindness to self can prevent shame from manifesting and affecting our self-identity. Kindness to self can help boost self-esteem and increase the feeling of confidence and optimism.

Being kind can be more manageable than being at the receiving end of kindness. Some of us are, at times, uncomfortable receiving kindness. Consider this example: Your colleague compliments you on some aspect, and you respond by saying, 'It's nothing'. Although we believe we are humble, the discomfort at having received kindness from another can make us negate the experience. Reactions that block receiving kindness, in turn, stop the power of the positive gesture. Instead, it is better to acknowledge or appreciate—'thank you for noticing' or 'thank you, I've been working very hard on this'—allowing the act of kindness to benefit both parties.

When you face challenges or experience failure, what is the tone of your self-talk? Is it friendly and soothing or hostile? If it is the latter, speaking to yourself as you would talk to someone you truly loved with kindness would lead to more self-concern and care.

Being kind in the workplace

Kindness strengthens relationships, developing community, solidarity, and increasing social cohesion. Acts of kindness can also offer fresh perspectives and act as an inspiration for others. Overcoming social conflict and enhancing social cohesion to achieve goals together is a core aspiration of any team; organisations, therefore, would benefit significantly by encouraging and practicing kindness within work cultures. Sharing responsibilities and opportunities with others, inspiring positive actions towards others, teaching empathy and compassion, and encouraging random acts of kindness among team members and managers can also enable kindness in the workplace through modelling.

Performing acts of kindness is not difficult or time-consuming. Regardless of however large or small, the scale of the action shows similar psychological, physical, and social benefits to all. Individuals can show kindness to others in the workplace, for example by really paying attention to another, being polite, offering support, and letting others help them.

Barriers to kindness

When beginning your journey to kindness, overcoming existing barriers (temporarily) can be a challenge. Some obstacles to kindness include external rewards, concern about being rebuffed, and a lack of confidence.

Some studies have observed that some specific situational factors can act as barriers to kindness. For example, research shows that good thoughts alone do not translate to positive actions and that the speed at which we live our daily lives can prevent helping and kindness to others. Furthermore, when there are larger groups of people, humans can experience bystander apathy when observing an incident and will wait, thinking others will help first. As a result, the likelihood of anyone helping can reduce even in front of a car accident (Ghosh, 2020).

Kindness can be a socially risky endeavour. It can make us feel foolish or taken advantage of, and it requires bravery to be kind. However, the benefits of kindness are far superior to the necessary momentary courage. Therefore, being aware of such situations and manifesting kindness in our and others' lives is the way forward.

Optimism

What is optimism?

It is a belief and attitude that leads to the person having a very positive outlook on life. The optimist is likely to see failure as a temporary event and a learning opportunity. They are prone to considering that they have more positive experiences overall compared to others. Optimists are realistic in their thinking and aspirations. Such individuals are also likely to accept responsibilities for mistakes and errors but do not dwell on them.

The signs of an optimist include feeling that the future holds good things, that life will work out for the best, and that they will handle any problems that may arise. Males are said to be more optimistic than females, but this difference disappears in economic downturns.

Some argue that being optimistic has a genetic component which is then influenced by environmental factors such as parental style, family culture, and education. Being optimistic can fluctuate and will be influenced by factors such as a person's confidence level and recent events.

The benefits of being an optimist

Research shows that there are significant benefits to being an optimist. They are more likely to be persistent and, therefore, more successful as they will address obstacles and problems. Optimists are less likely to experience stress and more likely to have healthy habits for coping with stress. They are said to have better physical health than pessimists.

Explanatory styles

As humans, we explain life using these categories: Do things change over time, or do they remain stable? Is a given situation linked to one part of your life or all of it? Are events caused by you or external factors?

An optimist is likely to consider that positive events happen because of their own actions and qualities. These are seen as evidence that more encouraging episodes will occur in the future. Negative events will not be seen as their fault but as rare occurrences.

Conversely, a pessimist will feel that positive events happen by chance, are caused by external factors, and that they are responsible for negative events.

Difficulties associated with optimism

If someone's optimism is excessive, then they are at risk of optimism bias, so they will underestimate the probability of experiencing negative outcomes. They may then use unsafe behaviours and be less likely to take actions to mitigate the potential threats.

An optimist could also show toxic positivity. They will overvalue positive feelings and either ignore or suppress negative ones. This is not a beneficial approach. They may also disrespect the emotions experienced by someone who is in difficulty.

Optimism and work

Losada et al. investigated the impact of negative emotions at work. They observed company meetings through two-way mirrors and analysed statements and behaviours. They found that high performance teams were six times more likely to make positive statements, were more flexible and resilient, and were less likely to be mired in self-absorption and defensive behaviours.

Leadership IQ, in a survey of 11,308 employees, found that the level of optimism displayed by an employee was a good predictor of engagement, as was the resilience and assertiveness of the employee. However, of those surveyed, only 13% reported a high level of optimism and 33% reported low or moderately low levels.

Encouraging optimism

At the end of each day, stop and reflect on only the positives and successes experienced.

Reframe your thinking, if you are pessimistic, through cognitive re-structuring. Keep a diary for a week and identify those situations or events or people that trigger negative thinking. What is the evidence for this negative thinking? How can you replace the negative thinking with a more positive approach? For example, instead of thinking that you always become negative when stressed, why not learn about relaxing and breathing properly, and select a positive statement to say when you feel yourself becoming negative, e.g. I will manage.

Respect

This is a quality that most value, offer, and seek in all aspects of life. The Oxford English Dictionary defines it as the 'feeling of admiration for someone or something because of their excellent qualities or achievements'. Respecting another person means you value their perspectives, words and actions. Similarly, self-respect is a 'feeling of being proud of yourself and that what you do, say, etc. is right'. It is possible to tolerate someone without respecting them.

We learn respect through observing and interacting with others in work and life. It is shown by the words and actions that people use when relating to each other. Children and adults easily learn this skill unless the person has some qualities linked to Asperger's. People with Asperger's may find it more difficult to learn vicariously about abstract issues such as respect without it being shown to them in more direct ways.

How respect is demonstrated and valued can vary from culture to culture and it is important to be aware of these as we live in a multicultural world. Colleagues in Sri Lanka will use Anna's title as a sign of respect, even though they know her as a friend. This rarely happens in England.

Ways of building respect

Some of us default to timidity, passivity, and submission. We lack self-confidence and under-value ourselves. This damages our ability to form relationships and engage effectively with others. We may find it hard to share and think about our emotions or change or find it hard to deal with problems. Our desire to avoid confrontation and stay under the radar results in our opinions and capacities being dismissed rather than respected by colleagues and peers. We may be prone to anxiety, depression, and disassociation.

To address these issues, we need to recognise and understand the triggers that cause us to respond in a particular way. We need to acknowledge and express how we feel in situations, challenge our default instincts, and work at consciously changing the way we react to circumstances. We may need to force ourselves to speak up when we'd much rather shrink away—building up an inner sense of personal power, autonomy, and self-value.

People will sense the quality of our self-esteem and then respond accordingly. We can change and increase our self-esteem if we want. We're unlikely to transform ourselves into confident extroverts overnight, but there are techniques that can help us.

> 'No can make you feel inferior without your consent.'
> —*Eleanor Roosevelt, First Lady*

At the outset, we need to recognise and resist our natural inclination to opt for short-term benefit. It's natural for us to choose to do what makes us feel comfortable or happy right now rather than what would be in our best interests in the longer term. Thus, we're more likely to put up meekly with relationships and circumstances that make us feel under-valued or overlooked, because speaking up and making changes seems such a difficult or risky thing to do. Alternatively, we may need to tone down our behaviour. Some of us can interact with others disrespectfully because we can, or we don't know what else to do.

There are actions we can take to boost our sense of Self and increase our courage, and they can lead to people respecting us more. Non-verbal actions such as using a confident and open body posture can help as well as acting as though you are confident. Verbal behaviour, such as using positive words, can also increase self-respect. It is equally important not to use negative words to describe yourself. Spend time with and learn from others who are confident.

Practice your way to a more confident Self. Picture yourself in the typical situations or conversations that make you feel under-valued and disrespected. Imagine how you'd like to respond if you were brave, confident, and assertive. Then use those responses in actual situations. You might be tentative and anxious at first but work towards that image of calm assertiveness that you've envisaged for yourself.

Honesty

Most of us think we are honest, according to Dan Ariely (2012), who has studied lying for some years. If you are honest, then there is an obligation to tell the truth and avoid lying deliberately. (It is interesting to note that some now are questioning the veracity of parts of Ariely's data.)

Honest people are direct, do not over-elaborate, and will not tolerate lying to themselves or anyone else. They know how to build meaningful relationships based on trust. However, there can be risks in being too honest.

What constitutes honesty will vary from person to person and, sometimes, depend on your upbringing, community, culture, and ensuing moral code. For example, if someone asks you for your opinion about their sub-standard work and you know they are emotionally fragile, would direct honesty be needed? If you have a tendency towards equivocation and vagueness, would you describe yourself as an honest person?

There are a few occasions when it will not be possible to be honest. For example, if you have a manager who is harassing you, if a colleague is vulnerable, or if there is a significant risk to life if you tell the truth.

People learn about the importance of honesty or its opposite from the people in their past and current life. The past will influence them, but they can choose, as adults, how to live.

Even if you are an honest person, there are likely to be times when you lie. It is the extent to which lying is part of your lifestyle that makes a difference.

The impact of honesty at work

It is necessary to create and maintain trust, both internally and externally. The risk of conflict reduces and there is often greater engagement and motivation with better creativity. The risk of breaking rules and regulations also decreases.

Building honesty at work

Suggestions include being positive and reserving judgement until it is the right time to speak. Holding yourself, whoever you are, accountable is vital, as is providing honest and respectful feedback and being available.

Letting people know you will support them if they make errors will help them be more honest and grow as employees. Coaching can be of assistance.

Dishonesty needs to be tackled so that staff know that honesty is needed and expected. Creating and maintaining feedback loops for learning and communication is important and these need to be operationalised properly. Having an anonymous system for reporting dishonest acts can help, but only if it is utilised with dignity.

Being known as an honest person can mean that people will trust you more and they will be more likely to want to have relationships with you. Honesty and its converse, lying, can influence a group or an organisation. Those who are honest tend not to please everyone and are not hypocritical.

Honesty can lead to increased personal integrity, a sense of security and happiness, and greater life satisfaction. It also aids personal well-being and decreases stress and anxiety because it won't be necessary to remember all the lies that were told.

Observing how others interact will help you work out who is mostly honest and who is not. In our personal lives, we can choose not to spend too much time around those who are dishonest, but this is not always possible at work. Sometimes, it is necessary to work with a dishonest person.

Transparency

Many think that transparency can be achieved by simply being willing to share information and doing this consistently. Staff will feel that they are engaged, and this will be enhanced by leaders being excellent communicators who are willing to share positive and negative information and receive feedback. Leaders need to be prepared, within reason, to disclose certain aspects, such as their values and sense of purpose.

Expectations will be managed and there is likely to be better performance, engagement, trust, creativity, and collaboration. The level of psychological safety will increase significantly. It is also important that leaders and managers work to maintain safety, otherwise the psychological contract between leaders and staff will be broken.

It can take time to develop a culture of openness and transparency. Staff may not initially trust the intention and expectation of those leading the culture change. It is worth considering how much is shared and with whom. Sharing all the information with everybody may lead to people feeling overwhelmed and, sometimes, very slow teamwork and decision making. There may also be much confusion and worry. For example, this can happen if pay grades and salaries are shared without consideration of the impact of this type of knowledge.

Some, unfortunately, may use the intention to be transparent and open as an opportunity for sabotage. It is therefore worth thinking about how encouraging further transparency will affect staff and the culture.

Alongside information sharing, it is important to get to know staff and managers, as this will reinforce the intention to be open. Let people know you are always willing to listen.

Humility

This has become a very popular competence in the world of leadership. It is a rare and valuable quality that many aspire to and say they possess, but very few do. People with humility will concentrate on their teams and guide them to achieve the goals and vision. They will be open and listen, share credit, learn from other people, and be willing to admit mistakes and then address them.

The humble leader will be very self-aware and inclusive of others, value-based and prepared to ask for help. Such leaders will not abuse their power and authority. They will focus on developing their staff. The presence and use of these qualities often leads to better trust and staff engagement, job satisfaction and performance, and lower turnover.

Dean Nitin Nohria (2016) identified three types of humility. Intellectual humility occurs when the person, despite being an expert, will acknowledge their limits of knowledge and learn from others. Having moral humility means that you are realistic and know that there will be times when you fail to be moral but will then strive to address the issue as soon as possible. And finally, there is personal humility—you are reluctant to talk about yourself and your accomplishments.

Being willing to be humble means that you are from a background where this has been encouraged as opposed to being too confident. Somewhere along the line, the humble person has learned to put others first and does this almost without thinking. 'We had almost finished the first course of our lunch and there were two pieces left of the favourite dish. Everyone wanted one of them but was unwilling to be the greedy person. Victoria, without thinking, simply took the pieces and cut them into four and so everyone had a portion.'

You can encourage your own humility by putting others first in discussions and actions. Praising others, not yourself, is key. Let others know you will listen. Stop and reflect on your own self-confidence and trust and how you can maintain them humbly. Be prepared to stop and reflect on your words, thoughts, emotions, and actions.

Well-being

The concept of well-being is extremely popular in most sectors in which organisations operate. It has many useful elements, but we can also see that well-being interventions have been used as a panacea for many things.

At the level of the individual person, well-being is a state that is encouraged and enhanced by healthy living and working. It is dependent on the state of the person's physical health and mental health. The major categories for well-being (recommended by Gallup) are career, community, physical, social, and financial. Gallup based these on over 70 years of research on the topic. Some also add a sense of purpose as an integral factor.

There is a continuum from well-being to mental health and then mental illness. People will move from one to another depending on what is going on in their life. Physical health often interacts with well-being and mental health.

People often have some areas of life in which they are satisfied regarding well-being and less so in other parts. Some will have concrete plans in each key area and will enact them regularly and consistently. This will help them cope with the pressures and worries of daily life, even in COVID times.

The extensive research on well-being, stress, and anxiety at work reveals the importance of looking after yourself in as many areas of life as possible realistically. Doing so will enable people to cope with and manage whatever life brings.

Someone's approach to well-being depends on a variety of factors, the extent to which self-care was promoted at home, and how it is reinforced and encouraged currently. 'I have relatives, some of whom live healthily and well and others who do not. I know that I am capable of both lifestyles. I incorporate these tendencies into my life by living as healthily as possible but allowing one day a week in which I can relax, not do any exercise, and eat what I want to (in moderation).'

The global COVID pandemic had an adverse impact on most people's well-being partly because of the associated fears and anxieties but also the fact there were fewer opportunities for maintaining well-being, e.g. being able to go for walks or the gym. As people regrouped and rethought their plans for life and health, some adjusted positively. Others, especially those who were vulnerable in terms of mental health, found it difficult to manage, more than they would have in 2019. The main issue was to maintain well-being comfortably so that daily routines and habits could provide the person with a framework for coping and life. It is highly likely that people's mental health will remain vulnerable even as the pandemic is being better managed.

Most corporations, regardless of sector, will have a well-being initiative for their employees, such as gym membership, webinars on mindfulness, stress management, etc. Many focus on physical well-being with less attention being given to the other categories. These are mainly directed at the individual employee and not parts of the organisation, which often impact staff. IOM (UN Migration Agency) devised a mechanism based on health and psychosocial risk data and the UN Sustainable Development Goals to enable teams to review collectively their current approaches to well-being and then design plans to enhance it. The key areas were Team (how the team worked, and what they did), Support (for each other and from managers), Coping (knowledge and use of coping strategies for well-being and mental health), Environment (physical, safety, and sustainability), Knowledge of available well-being and mental health services, Home and Personal Life (work-life balance, relationships, money), and Managers and Leaders (presence and use of leadership competences).

Some actions, post assessment, were the responsibility of the team, and others were handed over to senior personnel to address. Those who used this method reported that they liked it partly because it took the focus away from the person being responsible for their stress management.

Facilitating organisational well-being

As well as offering opportunities through well-being programmes and similar initiatives, it is very important that the organisation looks at other factors that contribute to well-being. The approach taken by managers can make or break how well employees feel and thus impact the work culture.

When staff can align their own sense of purpose with that of the organisation, it also helps. We explore this further in the book when we consider interventions.

Fair human resources policies that are properly implemented make a big difference. Avoiding favouritism or promoting people because of nepotism will aid collective well-being.

Enhancing personal well-being

This can be done by carrying out an audit of how you are living your life in each of the key areas, then identifying the core strengths and areas for change and using this knowledge to build and enact a plan. It is very important to create daily reminders to encourage yourself, setting an alarm for exercise or reflection.

Having a close friend or buddy to support you as you both enhance your self-care can be a great help. The quality of social relationships is vital. We have found them to be a good predictor of how a person will cope with stress. You don't need 500 friends, but one or two people who you know will be there to support no matter what.

If someone is not looking after themselves, then they could be more prone to anxiety, stress, and worry. This may lead them, especially if they are very stressed, to use more unhealthy coping habits such as substance misuse or seek the company of those who are also not looking after themselves. It is not clear why they choose these negative behaviours.

They can be encouraged to improve their well-being, but this needs to be done by someone they trust. They need to examine why they have selected not to look after themselves, e.g. low self-respect, just not making enough time. It is best if they choose small steps to increase their well-being rather than suddenly design a brand-new lifestyle, as it is likely that changing greatly will be too much and they could self-sabotage.

Integrity

It is often seen as a personality trait or quality that is present and leads to the person acting with honesty in line with their core values and principles. Such individuals are being morally responsible, and this facilitates a synergy between a person's internal values and external verbal and non-verbal behaviours.

Integrity is associated with positive acts. We need three steps: working out what is right and wrong; acting for the greater good, even if there is a personal cost; then being open and saying that you are acting from your understanding of the difference between right and wrong.

Learning more about personal integrity

As with other qualities that we have discussed in this chapter, people in our personal and professional lives shape and influence personal integrity from a young age. The environment in which we live and operate then reinforces our integrity or subjugates it.

We often walk around without really exploring our approach to integrity. It is worth taking time to stop and reflect. Take some time to write down your core values and purpose. Think of occasions in the past where you felt you showed true integrity and when you did not. What circumstances led to each decision and action? What have you learned so that you can enhance your integrity?

Behaviours that show integrity

We describe a person with integrity as having a range of qualities. These include being gracious and respectful. They take responsibility for their words and actions, will uphold their values instead of seeking personal gain, and are honest and helpful.

'Thanga is a very respected and loved aunt in her family. She is engaging, very intelligent and cares for one and all. She acts with integrity and strength in many quiet and effective ways. Sometimes, her influence is not noticed, but it has a great impact. After several untoward events in her country that led to distance and distrust between people of different religions, she quietly, with her church, contributed to reconciliation and trust-building efforts. She, despite being retired, helps other older relatives to have as much of a decent life as possible. She is one of the very few family members who cares for and keeps in touch with almost everyone.'

Integrity at work

Integrity at work is an important component that is often assumed to be present. It is sometimes, however, occasionally absent. The presence or absence of integrity will influence the behaviour of others and the overarching culture.

A manager or leader with integrity will not feel the need to assert their power just because they can. At their very best, such leaders will be powerful and enable others. They demonstrate 'power with' as opposed to 'power over' as described by Marc Gold. Ambassador William Lacey Swing (to whom the book is dedicated) was the Director General of IOM (UN Migration Agency) for two consecutive terms ending in 2018. He was respected for his integrity and inclusiveness. He treated everyone with courtesy and kindness and was extremely dedicated to the purpose of IOM, and this influenced his words and actions.

You can gain integrity at work and show it by being accountable for what you do, taking part readily and working hard, following policies within reason, respecting others even if you disagree with them, praising and giving credit, not taking part in gossip or spreading falsehoods, and being accountable for mistakes and not passing blame onto others.

There will inevitably be times when someone places their integrity on one side and does or says something they regret. The best thing to do, in these circumstances, is to admit the error, apologise and rectify as needed, and then return to being a person with integrity.

Diversity and inclusion

In this book, we use the phrase diversity and inclusion as well as the current popular one of diversity, equity, and inclusion (DEI). Our intentions are the same for both terms. We remember what Herb Lovett said when asked which term was most appropriate to describe people who used to be referred to as those with learning disabilities. He said that, first, we should ask the person and, second, that we would always have debates about terminology until we achieved equity.

The Oxford English Dictionary defines diversity as 'the quality or fact of including a range of many people or things and inclusion as the fact of being included'.

That we are diverse is a fact, but appreciating our diversity and differences and striving for inclusion are aspirations that have been present for many generations.

'When one sits in the hoop of the people,
one must be responsible because
All of creation is related.
And the hurt of one is the hurt of all.
And the honour of one is the honour of all.
And whatever we do affects everything in the universe.'
—*Lakota Instructions for Living.*
White Buffalo Calf Woman

Both diversity and inclusion are much more in the public eye these days because of events and movements that have had a global impact, such as #MeToo and #BlackLivesMatters. What is positive is that what was previously silent and endured is now being spoken about. People have more courage to share their experiences, both positive and negative. This has led to discomfort, which is perhaps inevitable for both speakers and listeners. However, as we learn to listen and understand each other more, we can shift our own perspectives to be more inclusive.

People who formerly were excluded are now being included in life and organisations. This is a journey that has many paths and steps. For example, we may invite someone with a difference to set up a support group for themselves in an organisation, but that is the only action that is taken. Others will do more and include, in as many aspects as possible, the perspectives and views of people who have been left out, e.g. a seat on the board of the organisation.

As human beings, we need to explore our own perspectives and learn to be more open and inclusive. When someone says 'Black lives matter', that statement needs to be honoured rather than saying, 'All lives matter'. While this latter phrase is true, saying it can show disrespect for the speaker who is talking about one group.

True diversity and inclusion remain aspirations, but we are making progress slowly but surely. 'I worked in a country where it was difficult for women to work. During a training session just for women employees, they informed me they did not feel that there was enough inclusion and appreciation of their gender. During the discussion, we realised that there had been some progress, the evidence being that we were all in a room, at work, talking together, which would not have been possible 50 years ago. However, we needed more.'

Some people have overt and obvious differences and others do not, and as societies, we need to provide the psychological environment where each person can feel comfortable with their difference in their own way. Sometimes our own biases and perceptions can impede having an open attitude and accompanying behaviours.

'We had been asked to do some diversity training for an organisation and made sure that the facilitators were also diverse. Felicita, the lead facilitator, had a physical difference which was not obvious, was African American, and nonbinary. Some staff from the organisation asked to meet one of the facilitators, as they had some concerns. They were people with physical differences, overt and otherwise. Felicita met the staff group and explained that the team had done their best to be inclusive and that there would be opportunities for participants to contribute fully from their various perspectives. After a lengthy discussion, the staff group was still dissatisfied until Felicita disclosed that she also had a physical difference which was not obvious. It was exactly at this point that the group relaxed and became more comfortable with the programme.'

Where do our perspectives come from?

As before, our upbringing, education, and current environments influence us in terms of diversity and in-clusion. Sometimes we can articulate our perspectives, but there will be issues of which we are unaware until we say or do something. 'I had been on holiday and had a lot of luggage. I had pulled a muscle in my back; I booked a car and driver to take me to the airport so that I would not have to carry the luggage. I had assumed that the chauffeur would be a man who could carry the suitcases, and I was disappointed when I got a call from the female driver who had been assigned to me. It shocked me as I thought I was gender fair.'

We can and should explore our own conscious and unconscious views and perspectives by reflecting on what we have said and done around differences. Even if we say that we are inclusive, we need to look for evidence in our lives that this is the case. What stereotypes do we hold about other groups of people? Some have questioned the need to let other people know which pronouns someone would like used to describe themselves.

You can explore your perspectives by thinking about how you have been inclusive or not in the last few months. As human beings, we live in ways that confirm our own perspectives, and this includes what we watch, read, and see. What did you say and do? Did you have any reactions to any articles in the media that spoke of diversity and inclusion? Which films do you watch? What have you learned about yourself?

Diversity and inclusion interventions in organisations

Common interventions include training, staff support groups, discussion groups, and developing policies and procedures. These are a good start but remain at the level of concept. You may help people think about diversity and inclusion while they are in the training or reading a policy, but there is no guarantee that they will then behave differently.

It is important to ask people what they will do differently in a sustained way. They may need help to think this through. How can what we have learned be embedded in daily practice? Perhaps this could be a behavioural goal for employees as part of their overall tasks.

A philosophy called Normalisation was created in the 1970s to help service providers think differently about services for people with learning disabilities/difficulties. (The term is clearly unfortunate as it implies that there is a need for conformity which is not true.) It was, however, extremely effective, and many institutions closed, and services were re-provided in community settings.

The creators of this movement not only developed the philosophy but also designed a method and training that helped participants learn the philosophy and then use the method to work out how to be and act differently when they returned to their workplaces. The lesson here is that people not only need to learn about concepts and models but also require help in implementing the same. Why not provide opportunities for continued discussion and learning from each other, or set behavioural goals as part of the annual appraisal?

David Bryan, Sonia Watson, and Emmicki Roos, in the Experts section (Chapter Five), have shared their views and perspective on diversity and inclusion and privilege. They speak from a base of solid experience and expertise.

Communication and building relationships

This is a vital skill and one that is necessary for the articulation of other behaviours. Effective communication means that you must learn to interact with others in a way that ensures that their voice is heard and noted. We hear others by what they say and their tone (approximately 30%) and what they do non-verbally, i.e. body language (70%). This may be why we experienced difficulties in 2020/2021, because of COVID, when we switched to remote working. Most of us forgot we can still pay attention to body language even though we could not sense the pheromones and hormones of the other person.

Patsy Rodenburg effectively describes three levels at which we communicate: Level One—we are internalised and effectively speaking to ourselves with minimal interaction with the other person; Level Two—we are engaged with and listen to the other person, and wait for them to finish speaking before considering how we will respond; Level Three—we are effectively talking at the other person with little consideration.

We learn our communication approaches and styles from many places: home, friends, school, and work. Our self-comfort and confidence also affect it, as well as stress levels. If we lack confidence and are very stressed, then it is likely that we could use Level One or Level Three behaviours.

You can enhance your communication by learning more, ideally through working with an actor who can give you live feedback on your interactions. Patsy Rodenburg's books contain many helpful exercises to improve breathing and voice use.

If you are working with someone who is not confident, then the first task is to help them relax, perhaps by slowing your movements and speaking more slowly. If your counterpart is someone who speaks at you, then it is important, through your behaviour, to influence them to beginning interacting appropriately with you.

Collaboration

Collaboration is 'the act of working with another person or group of people to create or produce something' (Oxford English Dictionary). Cooperation is similar but is less intense and has fewer expectations.

One of the best places to view collaboration in action is in the arts. There is an excellent YOUTUBE clip of Fred Astaire and Rita Hayworth dancing together while a Jackie Wilson song is playing. It is amazing to see how they are supporting and collaborating, and they are amicable. There are also many instances of partnership and synchrony in sports. *The Last Dance* documentary on Netflix has some fine examples of the synergy between the Chicago Bulls as they played basketball. In fact, synchronising was something that the team practised as guided by Phil Jackson (Head Coach).

Necessary qualities

Collaboration requires an ability to sense and interact with others in verbal and non-verbal ways. This means that you must be open, be willing to listen and sense the other person or group.

Trust between collaborators is vital, as is the ability to communicate clearly. A reluctance to share will not help. Being someone who is trustworthy and has faith in others is important. There are two types of trust: cognitive trust which includes a belief that others are capable, dependable and can collaborate; and emotional trust which assumes that others will care for us. Cognitive trust is easy to assume, but it is emotional trust that takes time. Senior leaders can encourage emotional trust by being empathic and self-disclosing in a positive and non-threatening way (Neeley, 2021).

Collaboration is built by taking time to get to know others, having a common aim and the capabilities to achieve the goals, and being willing to be flexible. Some say that common rules for interaction can be helpful.

In business

Effective collaboration maximises success and can lead to healthier work relationships and workflow. Productivity and efficiency improve, as does problem solving. However, it is important to maintain a little distance and not become too cohesive, as this can create conformity in thinking and a decrease in creativity. The physical or virtual space in which people work will also affect the degree to which people feel they can collaborate. Johan Schaar explores collaboration and cooperation further in his section in Chapter Five.

Happiness

The Oxford English Dictionary defines happiness as 'the quality or condition of being happy', and the word happy as 'the state of pleasurable contentment of mind; deep pleasure in or contentment with one's circumstances'.

We see largely that it is a state as opposed to a trait. However, common sense shows that happiness can be more than momentary. Some argue that there is a strong genetic component and others say that it is an interaction between genetics and environment which is more likely.

Martin Seligman states that happiness comprises positive emotions and activities and that there are three categories of happiness. Positive emotions, linked to the present, include pleasure and gratification, some of which can be transitory. Joyful emotions, linked to the past, include satisfaction and contentment, pride, and serenity. And those linked to the future include hope, trust, and optimism.

Being happy can lead to some positive consequences. Those who are deemed to be happy are more likely to be successful and have a better support system and network of friends. Happy people are also reported to cope better in life, be a positive influence, give more to charity, and be more helpful. Overall, there is a positive and strong correlation between happiness and mental health. This applies regardless of gender.

There are some indications that there may be cultural differences depending on whether a culture is individualistic or collective. However, this is still being investigated.

Dr Tal Ben-Shahar suggests that there are four approaches to life: Egocentric/Hedonic approach and the Rat Race approach, both of which are very self-oriented. The person will seek happiness and pleasure for themselves; Nihilistic approach—the individual is very pessimistic and likely to succumb to stress; and the Positive approach—where the person aims to be happy, has good self-care, can cope, and is supportive of others.

People can also be self-happy with high self-esteem and confidence. Such individuals will be good at self-care (eating well, maintaining physical and mental health, sleeping well, managing stress). They are likely to be grateful, compliment others, and have effective social supports. People like this will take responsibility for their actions and learn from their mistakes.

Happiness at work

Happy people are much more productive, and they are more likely to maintain good health and positive relationships. All these lead to greater success at work and increased likeability and decreased stress.

Courage

Courage has been described as an intentional act that is usually carried out after consideration. It poses significant risk to the actor and is inspired by a desire to be noble regardless of any fears (Rate et al., 2007). Sometimes, the courageous thing is not to act. Courage, according to Aristotle, lies somewhere between cowardice and rashness (Ashton, 2017). Courage has been said to be synonymous with being fearless.

Different types of courage are described in the literature: physical (being fearful but still taking action); spiritual (living with purpose, perhaps through faith); intellectual (ready to be more open); emotional (following your heart); moral (being willing to advocate for what is right); social (being prepared to be yourself in adverse social situations); and psychological (willingness to look at your Self honestly).

Usually, we need a catalyst to be courageous. There is some debate about the role that fear plays in triggering courageous behaviour. A certain amount of fear is needed, but not so much that it is overwhelming. Others also suggest that integrity is a key element of being courageous.

Being courageous at work can be an advantage in small and large ways. Usually, the tempo for this is set by the leader of the group or organisation. Detert (2021) notes that there does not seem to be a specific trait that promotes courage, thus most can be brave. It is worth starting small if practicing being courageous and thinking about feelings before, during, and after the act of bravery.

Courage can be developed through practice and example. It can also be influenced by others in your past and current life and the circumstances in which you operate. If an organisation has become very risk averse, then it will be more difficult to be courageous. Some people, because of their background, may remain fearful and not feel able to be courageous.

Exploring past actions can also assist to enhance the tendency to be courageous. Looking at what helped and what did not when you last tried to be brave can increase your approach to courage.

Shadow behaviours, thoughts, and emotions

Here are descriptions of the most common shadow behaviours, thoughts, and emotions that we have encountered. This is not an exhaustive list but a start. Please remember that most of us have the potential to demonstrate and use most of these behaviours. This is an opportunity for all of us to learn about our shadow sides and then consider how to be more positive.

It is worth being cautious when exploring shadow behaviours, thoughts, and emotions, as they have clearly served a purpose, even if it is negative. Choosing to look at and perhaps alter or let go of these behaviours needs to be done after you understand why the person is using them, and the person must be prepared to change (Richard Schwartz).

Compassion fade/fatigue

This occurs most frequently in human services such as health and social care and the humanitarian sector, especially for those who work directly with those who receive services and are in dire need, such as migrants, refugees, and very ill people. Professionals working in direct care human services often have great compassion and care and they give of themselves freely. However, they sometimes must help and work with people who are at the worst points of their lives and may have been through trauma, e.g. disaster survivors. Given that just listening to or reading about another's trauma has an emotional effect on the listener or reader, then it should not be surprising when these professionals develop compassion fade or fatigue. Here, the person almost stops caring and 'tunes out' as described by Paul Slovic. They become less empathic as a coping mechanism.

People with compassion fade/fatigue are likely to feel exhausted, irritable, forget how to look after themselves, and self-medicate, etc. Sometimes the best option is for the person to leave their work for a while (one to three months), rest and regroup, perhaps see a counsellor and then come back to work with a more effective range of coping strategies, good social support, and better self-care. Some, however, leave the sector and take up something else.

Hypocrisy

This is the antithesis of integrity and is seen when someone claims to have and use their morals and standards but does not. An example is Prime Minister Boris Johnson, who publicly advocated for the use of masks during Euro 2020 but was photographed shortly afterwards not wearing one when he should have.

Jung argues that being hypocritical is an opportunity for the shadow side to emerge. While this is true for some, it is also possible that there are other reasons. A timid person may be hypocritical to survive being in a strenuous life or work situation, e.g. saying that they agree with a project proposal made by a domineering manager as they want to keep their job. Some may not realise that they are being hypocritical or are because the work or community culture demands it.

Some will avoid being hypocritical because of having to cope with the dissonance that will arise when they are. Having been duplicitous, they must reconcile their deeds with their sense of Self including values, and for some, this can be difficult.

To dissuade yourself from being hypocritical, it is worth reflecting on your own moral code and exploring its boundaries. What would be acceptable transgressions and what would not? Decide on a line that you will not cross, as it will mean that you are being hypocritical.

If you are and have been hypocritical, how will you reconcile this with how you see yourself? To whom do you need to apologise?

Lying/dishonesty

Most of us know how to lie and have done so in our lives. 'For example, I took a break from writing just now and emailed a friend to say that I had sent her vegetables and other healthy food for her birthday present. I did it as a joke as I had posted chocolates which she loves. But it was a lie that I had written. Does this matter in the grand scheme of life? Probably not, but it could also be a reminder to me of the slippery slope of lying if I then began to lie in more important areas.'

People will lie for many reasons. A desire for material gain can motivate lies, although there probably will be negative consequences such as getting caught, e.g. claiming to have a damaged lottery ticket. If a person lies out of self-interest, then their behaviour can become a social norm and it can be contagious, e.g. describing a leader as fantastic even if they are not but are instead very controlling and target those who do not praise them. Lying can be encouraged in some organisations and even lead to financial rewards.

There are, however, consequences of lying, even if it makes you feel better. It can deplete you both emotionally and cognitively. You may stop thinking of yourself as a good person and you may be less trusted.

Sometimes we lie for compassionate reasons (pro-social lying) and, if we do, then it is possible that people will understand and see us as still trustworthy and moral, e.g. saying a colleague looks fantastic even if they are dressed poorly because they are nervous and just about to go into a very important meeting.

Lying is often accompanied by micro expressions and these give the person away, e.g. not looking at the speaker, talking too much. Men are said to lie more than women and younger people more than older. People behave more dishonestly when rejected. Very few will lie and cheat to pathological levels, most will lie and cheat a little. (Van der Zee et al., 2016)

When does it occur?

Dishonesty is reported to fluctuate during the day—we are more likely to lie at the end of the day as we become more depleted, thus lowering our moral awareness and self-control. Lying is more likely if we are in situations that facilitate it, such as seeing someone else lie.

There can be a tension between wanting to be a good person versus wanting the benefits of dishonesty, and this will lead to ethical dissonance. If you are effective at justifying dishonest behaviour and still feel good or even better about yourself, then you may be more likely to be behave dishonestly in the future.

How to stop

Lying can be discouraged by taking time to see yourself as a moral person and by having a desire to think of yourself positively. What can you learn from your past actions? When were you honest? What can you do to be more honest? What needs to be forgiven?

If you are trying to help someone who is lying, it is important to help them feel comfortable before talking to them about their behaviour. How can you help them relax? Think about how lying became normal for that person. What happened in their history, work, or otherwise? What maintains the behaviour? What has it done to their self-esteem and respect? Having helped the person understand themselves a little more, then discuss what other behaviours they could adopt to reinforce their self-esteem and respect in a more positive way.

Prejudice and discrimination

Prejudice refers to the holding of an unjustified and often inaccurate attitude about an individual or group based on what is their defining characteristic, such as race, culture, or gender fluidity. Discrimination encompasses behaviours (verbal and non-verbal) that are often used against that group about whom the person is prejudiced.

Discrimination is often present, and it is an interesting shadow in all our lives. Few use direct discrimination these days. 'My most recent example was in a supermarket in Switzerland in 2019. I was waiting in line to check out and the cashier insisted on telling only the non-white customers (ahead of me) that they had to show her all the contents of all their shopping bags before she would serve them. These were bags containing items purchased legitimately from other shops. When I brought up this issue with the store managers, they said that they weren't sure if this was discriminatory behaviour.'

Nowadays, it is usually indirect discrimination of people with differences and that makes it harder to name it. Here are some examples: speaking in French to a staff member in a French store and that person's focus was on correcting the customer's grammar rather than serving them. A staff member at a post office, rather than explaining to the diverse customer why it was necessary to complete a form in a particular way, said that they must not understand 'our rules'. These are microaggressions which have been extensively researched by Professor Derald Wing Sue.

Findings from the American Psychological Association's 2015 Stress in America survey showed that those who had faced discrimination rated themselves as more stressed than those who had not faced it. It could also contribute to the development of anxiety, depression, obesity, high blood pressure, and substance misuse. Discrimination occurs most often in the workplace.

The anticipation of discrimination can also lead to stress, which may negatively affect the ability to function in the workplace. The person may avoid some situations as they foresee that discrimination may occur.

Discriminatory practices affect job satisfaction, motivation, commitment, loyalty, and additionally staff turnover is likely to be higher. It can affect reputation and recruitment and it increases liability, as it is illegal in most jurisdictions.

Dealing with discrimination

It is important to focus on and remember the strengths you possess and your successes. Make sure that you have a strong and supportive network of people.

When you can, reflect on what was said and how you responded. What was good and what would you like to have done differently? Perhaps rehearse with a trusted friend how you would handle a similar situation in the future.

If you are someone who discriminates

If you have recognised this quality in yourself, stop and think about what your rationale and evidence is for justifying your beliefs and behaviours. Sometimes, people develop biases and associated behaviours because of fear of a supposed unknown or they may have learned it from a family member or at school or work. Alternatively, they could have picked up their views from the media. It is important to assess what is in the media for veracity and accuracy.

When we act negatively towards another person, we often don't think about the impact of our behaviours and actions on the person or group who has been targeted. If we did, we probably would not carry out the behaviour. Thus, it is vital to stop and think about how you would feel if someone behaved as you had.

Sometimes, discrimination has a protective function, or it could mean that you want to be seen as part of a group. If this is true, then what else could you do to feel comfortable or be part of the group?

Having reflected, would you be prepared to change? What help will you need? Which alternative words and behaviours could you rehearse and use? David Olusoga suggests that learning more about other members of our world can be helpful. How will you remind yourself to be more positive?

It is worth all of us exploring our views and perspectives to consider whether we could discriminate without recognising it. 'As part of a training session, we asked participants to share all the stereotypes that they knew about people from other nationalities. It was amazing how quickly participants could answer this question.'

What views and stereotypes do you have about people who are or could be different? How do they influence how you think about them and interact? What is positive and negative about your approach? What needs to change?

Hubris

Hubris, as a psychological concept, was most recently articulated by Owen and Davidson (2009). They collated a range of behaviours that can be seen in leaders with substantial power, which is a necessary condition. The actions include excessive self-confidence accompanied by a disregard for advice or criticism from others. Individuals with hubris are focussed on their own self-image and glorification and they can be reckless and impulsive. They are not that connected to reality, believe they can do no wrong, and can be cruel. People with hubris override anyone's else's vision or suggestion and consider that they will be vindicated, regardless.

Such people can be charming, persuasive, willing to take risks, and have an overabundance of self-confidence. Conversely, they can be incompetent, not pay enough attention to detail, fail to listen to others, have clouded judgement, make poor decisions, and have an impaired use of morals.

It is an acquired condition which only arises when a person is in power. It is then maintained by repetition of behaviours both from the person and those around them. Tourish (2020) states that these actions, and the associated social field that is created, reinforce the persona of hubris. It can and usually diminishes with the loss of power. UK Prime Ministers, US Presidents, and CEOs, amongst others in similar positions, are prone to hubris.

It is very unlikely that those with hubris will seek professional help. There are, however, interventions that can be used to alleviate its impact. At the individual level, this includes ensuring self-control and self-evaluation, paying attention to others' needs, and allowing others to give you accurate feedback. At the organisational level, increased accountability, effective performance appraisal systems, and oversight mechanisms (internal and external) are needed, as well as term limits.

Jealousy and envy

Jealousy and envy have some similarities and occur when someone covets what 'belongs' to another, e.g. a partner or an object or position. Both probably stem from personal insecurities and can lead to the same outcomes as other emotions, such as resentment and anger.

Some argue that it is a necessary emotion because it can motivate someone to preserve a relationship. While this has some validity, jealousy can be very wearing on the recipient.

Symptoms of jealousy can include being preoccupied with the issue, to the exclusion of all else, and physical signs such as raised heart rate and sweating. Jealousy and envy can occur both at home and work. It usually does not have a positive impact on the person who is the focus.

Research suggests the causes of envy and jealousy include insecurity (poor self-esteem), feeling threatened, fear of abandonment, and having trust issues. They can lead to controlling behaviour, damage relationships, and increase insecurity.

If someone is jealous or envious, they may have developed a rationale and justification for their feelings and behaviours. These can vary in severity and intensity, as well as the extent to which they are real, valid, and rational.

Coping starts with stopping and assessing why you are jealous or envious. What is the validity for those feelings? What is the evidence of their existence? Why did the feeling arise? How can you re-direct your feelings and energies into something more positive? For example, instead of resenting a colleague who has just been promoted, why not look at your CV and plan what you can do to enhance your chances of promotion?

If someone is jealous or envious of you, how valid is this feeling? How did you contribute, if at all? How can you engage with the person and develop a different relationship?

Pessimism

'The attitude that things will go wrong, and that people's wishes or aims are unlikely to be fulfilled.'
(American Psychological Association)

Pessimists are likely to expect the negative and become suspicious if the opposite occurs. Signs of a pessimistic attitude include feeling surprised when things work out, thinking that the risks outweigh any benefits, focusing on flaws, engaging in negative self-talk, and assuming all good things will end.

A range of factors can lead to such attitudes and include family history and other social and environmental issues. Some also state that there is a genetic component. Pessimism and its counterpart, optimism, both influence people's cognitions including thinking style. You may feel helpless and could be prone to greater stress and have fewer coping skills.

You could be prepared for the worst, but this may adversely affect you and you could have lower self-esteem and be more prone to anxiety and depression. Pessimistic employees can have more negative attitudes, and this can affect productivity, leading to lower motivation and limited work ethics. As a result, a blame culture could develop.

The cognitive strategy of defensive pessimism is used by some to anticipate and plan for the what ifs. People who use this strategy can have lower self-esteem and higher levels of anxiety. They set low expectations. Conversely, a strategic optimist will expect that there will be a good outcome, not have detailed plans, and won't be very anxious.

Other ways of addressing a pessimistic attitude include learning to hope for the best and plan for the worst, labelling negative thoughts, being realistic, and testing any fears by looking for evidence.

Competitiveness

Being competitive can be helpful, and it has a function. It can lead to greater effort and better performance via physiological and psychological activation. However, its impact depends on the feelings that arise. If people are fearful and anxious, then they could also be less creative and more unethical. If they feel positive and excited, then they could be inventive and more principled.

Positive competition also encourages the use of skills and talents without threat. It also unlocks potential and focuses on capability and achievement for all.

How competition makes employees feel is the key. Some competitions elicit fear and anxiety because they are based on threat. If people are anxious, they are less likely to choose innovative behaviours and more likely to be unethical. Others can focus on winning a coveted bonus. This can lead to anticipation and excitement; they are more likely to be ingenious and less likely to be unethical.

When collaboration turns into negative competition, sabotage is much more likely. In extreme competitiveness, the focus shifts from achieving the goal to stopping others. It may lead to decreased effectiveness and an increase in the time for project completion.

Very competitive people only think of the short term because they value winning over efficiency. External factors often motivate hyper-competitive people. If someone has high inner self-esteem though, then they are less likely to be competitive.

If someone is competitive, it is important to think of ways of collaborating, but it may be useful to be wary of trusting the person while continuing to be professional.

If you are competitive, it is worth asking what purpose it serves and whether it encourages trust and co-operation. What else could you do to have more collegial relationships?

Revenge

Some will say that revenge is a response to being treated unjustly. You could also be jealous or feel the need for retaliation. You want to make the other person suffer or you want them to stop.

Forty-four percent of employees who completed a survey (450 in total), admitted to exacting revenge on a co-worker, e.g. spreading rumours, hiding possessions, getting someone fired, sabotage, tampering with equipment, eating their food, using information gained from social media, deleting work (Insurance Quotes, 2018). This occurred at all levels of seniority. Reasons for taking revenge included 'making me look bad, was rude or disrespectful, insulting, abused their power, spread rumours, took credit for my work'. Eighty-three percent of the respondents said that there were no real repercussions. A few said that they had received a written warning or were suspended or fired.

As noted above, actions taken to be vindictive can involve the use of social media. Work-related retaliation includes giving a poor performance appraisal, bullying, harassment, spreading rumours, blaming, and threats. Smaller actions such as purposely not doing what was agreed are also possible.

An inflated social confidence and sense of entitlement could produce a desire to take revenge. Neurotics who are likely to ruminate on issues and have experienced anger and hostility can seek revenge years later. You could strive for revenge if you feel you have been rejected socially. However, if you tend to forgive, then you are less likely to seek revenge.

People often feel justified in their actions, and such justification can give momentary pleasure, assuage anger, and prove power. Taking revenge does not always lead to the person feeling better and could also lead to greater anxiety and the risk of retaliation. It is rarely cathartic; the person often continues to focus on the transgressor and the act, especially if they have taken revenge as opposed to witnessing it.

People include revenge in their repertoire if they have seen or experienced it in their life. They will find a way of justifying such behaviour and this belief may not be evidence based.

If you come across someone who is prone to such actions, then it is important to be careful about engaging with them while remaining professional. It is important to learn to recognise the signs of these individuals such as them taking an intense dislike to someone else with little justification and saying things like, 'I'll get them, wait."

Taking revenge, while perhaps satisfying in the short term, rarely solves much. Perhaps think about what made you take revenge: what was the evidence for feeling that you had to, and how could you address the issue in a more positive way?

Psychopathic and sociopathic behaviours at work

Psychopathy and sociopathy are two subgroups of antisocial personality disorders in the Diagnostic and Statistical Manual (DSM 5) which is used to assess people for mental illnesses. There are some differences between the two, largely in terms of the degree to which the behaviours described below are used.

The expected behaviours include being someone who does not respect social norms or laws. Such people are prone to lying and deceiving, using false identities, being aggressive, and they may not consider their own safety. They are very unlikely to feel or show guilt or remorse sincerely. Such individuals are also seen as cold, manipulative, attempting to control others, and may misuse substances. They may have multiple personas. People with these diagnoses may have limited social skills and find it difficult to manage their anger.

In the work setting, they can be charming to more senior people but abusive to subordinates. They can bully simply because they know how to and are said to enjoy using the associated behaviours. It is estimated that one percent of the general population could be diagnosed as psychopathic and three to four percent in business.

People who could be categorised as successful business psychopaths are said to be more conscientious. This quality is less present in psychopaths who are criminal. Psychopaths can be very charming, have an inflated sense of self, and are good at manipulating others.

Research, based on those who are within forensic services, indicates that people who could be diagnosed as psychopaths often have traumatic upbringings. It is unclear if this also applies to those in the business sector, as they are often sub-clinical and undiagnosed.

There is also, often, a big difference between those in the business sector who show these qualities and those who need help from mental health and forensic services and with similar labels and that is the severity of their actions. Behaviours used in the business sector are often low intensity, high impact, and high frequency in nature, e.g. harassment, mobbing, and continued fraud. Those shown by people with similar tendencies and who use mental health and forensic services are usually high intensity, high impact, and low frequency, such as murder and paedophilia.

It is extremely difficult to help someone with these behaviours change. The success rate is very low. If someone acknowledges that they have these qualities, then they need to be helped by very experienced mental health professionals.

If you are working with someone who has these qualities, it is important not to take their behaviour personally. It is vital to maintain a professional relationship but also to be assertive with the person in a polite and non-threatening way so that they cannot intimidate.

Machiavellianism

It is a personality trait, and the salient features are indifference in terms of morality and being manipulative and callous. The emphasis is on gaining and keeping power by whatever means necessary and planning to achieve personal goals. People high in this characteristic lack morals, appear cold, and are low in emotional empathy and recognition but not necessarily in emotional intelligence. They will achieve at the expense of others and may not realise the exact effect of their actions. Those with these qualities may not have much insight into their own emotions and may not feel guilt.

Machiavellians function well when there is ambiguity and/or competition. They can initially appear charming. They do not have to be the centre of attention and may prefer being in the background so they can be manipulative. Such individuals are likely to use very negative management approaches.

They are more likely to lie and fabricate in job interviews. At work, they are prone to not share information; they can be arrogant, dominant, and are feared. Research has found that there is a strong correlation between the presence of Machiavellianism and bullying. Individuals with these qualities are also said to function well in political settings.

They will have built these qualities over the years. It is possible that the person has learned them by seeing others, in their childhood or work environment, use these behaviours. They may then feel that these actions are their best option, partly because that is all they know. It is, again, unclear if there is a genetic component. It is possible that someone with Machiavellian qualities could change with support, but they would first need to own the behaviours and acknowledge their impact on others.

It is worth being wary of working with or for someone with these competences. You can manage by setting boundaries and being appropriately assertive. Ensure that you look after yourself and build alliances with others in the same situation to support each other but not try to counter the negative actions that are presented.

Show and use positive healthy behaviours regardless of those being used by the person with Machiavellian qualities. Be careful about sharing personal or confidential information, as they may use this against you.

Narcissism

It is a human characteristic where the person is extremely self-centred in their own needs, concerns, and appearance at the expense of all else. Some behaviours shown include a sense of entitlement, arrogance, selfishness, and a lacking in concern for others. This is the person who will, if you seek solace from them, turn the discussion to themselves. Sometimes narcissism is a protection for low self-esteem, i.e. an over-compensation. Narcissism, in excess, can be damaging for the narcissist.

The characteristic has similar symptoms to narcissistic personality disorder (classified as a mental illness) but the difference is in severity and impact on life. People diagnosed as having narcissistic personality disorder can find it extremely difficult to function in life (personal and work).

As usual, there is speculation about the causes of narcissism. Some say there are genetic reasons, others argue for the role of environmental factors or a combination of both. Some suggest that parenting style can have an effect—either excessive adoration or criticism.

Some qualities of narcissism can be helpful when becoming a leader, but they can also lead to failure, e.g. not taking others' needs or views into account. Narcissistic employees, if they feel their self-esteem is threatened, may engage in negative behaviours and thoughts, e.g. thinking that others are out to get them. Narcissistic managers and staff will seek external material validation at work such as having large offices or a huge company car. They often look for constant affirmation, which can be draining.

People with narcissism can be supported by seeking professional help, but for that to work, they need to acknowledge that they need it. If you are working with someone with these qualities, then it would help to set boundaries and provide proportionate support.

Self-sabotage

Self-sabotage is 'the act of destroying or undermining something, often covertly and directed at yourself' (Mindtools). The behaviours used include procrastination, comfort eating, deliberate self-harm, chronic lateness, and not delivering on time. These can be accompanied by negative self-talk.

The person carrying out these behaviours may or may not be aware that they are using them. They may have low self-esteem and could be uncomfortable with any actions or events that could elevate them. They could carry out the self-sabotage to continue having a negative perspective of themselves.

People with a background of abuse can self-sabotage, even if they have had professional help. They may be fearful of success or of letting people become too close to them. They may prefer to maintain their current status. Sometimes, people who are extremely stressed and have become rigid in their thinking may carry out some actions to sabotage themselves, e.g. saying something rude, apologising and then being rude again to the person who accepted their apology.

If you are someone who does self-sabotage, then please stop and learn more about what triggers you. How do you feel immediately after you have sabotaged yourself? How could you change your response to the triggers? What can you do to focus on your more positive attributes? What could be your plan to change and stop self-sabotaging?

Working with someone who self-sabotages can be tiring, irritating, and make you feel sad. Above all, it is important to be supportive of the person and praise them realistically and not effusively. We should not try to help them analyse their actions, as this could lead to a conflict of interest because there may be some deep underlying issues.

Underperformance

Underperformance occurs for a variety of reasons as opposed to laziness on the person's behalf, as is often assumed. They may be under pressure at home, have physical or mental health problems, or be experiencing harassment and bullying at work. Whatever the reason, underperforming usually places the person under severe stress, especially if they are working in a competitive or high-risk environment.

They may have been employed to do a job that is beyond their capabilities, e.g. being expected to produce written work in a language in which they are not proficient. A few may deliberately underperform as retaliation because they consider that they have been slighted or not respected.

The first step is to be very sure that the person is underperforming and then have a discussion with them. It is worth taking time in the conversation and reassuring the person that the intention is to help, not punish. Ask them what issues may contribute to their underperformance and how the organisation can help. Once this has happened, then there is a duty to help the person get the support they need in a consistent manner.

If the person has deteriorating physical health or mental health or underlying neuropsychological problems (difficulties reading, writing, etc.), they will need a proper assessment, treatment and social support, and a good return to work plan. The person needs to be helped by health professionals first. Managers should only be involved as needed.

Occasionally, the person may find it difficult to trust you, especially if they are being bullied. It would be worth asking them to talk to someone from the internal justice system or the staff representative if they do not want to speak to you (if one exists).

They may have misunderstood expectations of the role or find it difficult to meet them. As they are employees, it is important to help them consider the expectations and then work out what extra support or education is needed.

If you are underperforming, it usually better to stop and think about why and what help you may need. We all have times when we have underperformed, and it is worth pausing to consider what you can do rather than just trying to carry on and making yourself worse.

Bullying and harassment

The UK Government defines bullying and harassment as 'behaviour that makes someone feel intimidated or offended' that can 'happen face to face, by letter or email or phone'. Harassment is usually linked to a person's diversity, such as age or disability or sexual or gender orientation or religious belief.

There are usually laws in place to address the use of these behaviours that can include deliberate aggression from shouting to constantly criticising someone, withholding resources, spreading rumours, abuse of authority, and denying promotion. These behaviours can be carried out by an individual or a group in which case it is known as mobbing, which can be relentless.

Most of us could bully if we wanted to, but most of us choose not to. It is worth remembering this as you read on.

Impact of being bullied

If these behaviours are used, they may start gradually but can, if not addressed, become continuous and relentless. There needs to be a workplace culture that facilitates the use of these aggressive behaviours.

The impact of these behaviours can be significant even if they are low in intensity, such as occasional negative comments about work performance made by a manager in quarterly supervision. Obviously, if such behaviours are more frequent and intense, then their impact can be massive, especially if there is cyberbullying.

The recipient of these behaviours is likely to experience a wide range of emotions, such as helplessness, increased vulnerability, anger/frustration and shock, and lowered confidence. They may also have physical and psychological symptoms, for example, inability to sleep, headaches, panic, anxiety, stress, family tension, poor concentration, and low morale and productivity.

The workplace is also often affected by increased absenteeism, staff turnover, and costs for providing psychosocial support when these actions are addressed. There is also likely to be decreased productivity and motivation, lower morale, a reduced corporate image, and less customer confidence.

Bullies and harassers seem to be able to identify individuals who are not confident, are unassertive, and are vulnerable. Occasionally, however, they will select someone who is confident but poses a perceived threat.

Qualities

Why does someone use these behaviours? Some are insecure in themselves and may not know how else to manage or lead. It is a way of demonstrating power and is an effective tactic to get what they want. They might not know how to or want to manage in a more democratic, kind, and compassionate manner. Bullies are also likely to be able to morally disengage from their actions (Moore, 2015). They rarely think of the impact of their behaviours on another and if the recipient becomes upset, they are unlikely to acknowledge their role in eliciting that emotion.

Such individuals could have had a traumatic upbringing or work life after which they have normalised these behaviours as being acceptable. They could be envious or resentful. For example, 'I really don't like Corinne, she is so full of herself.' They may use bullying as a protection against some imagined fear.

How to help a bully

Ideally, there should be a substantive range of policies and procedures as well as an operational internal justice system in place. The policies should be descriptive and state what is needed to address such behaviours as well as what should be done to prevent their occurrence. And, crucially, these policies should be used and not just listed in the policy manuals. Internal justice systems should be trustworthy, otherwise staff will not approach them. Similarly, there should be a body that represents staff to whom staff members can go to for advice. All these interventions need to have full and proper support from leaders and managers.

It is important that bullying is tackled properly, that the survivor is given the help they need, and that they feel safe. Otherwise, the chances of healing and recovery for the survivor are small.

Helping someone who bullies can be very difficult, as it is very unlikely that anyone will have approached them on this issue. Therefore, they have received tacit reinforcement for their behaviours and feel that they can continue. Hence, it is very unlikely that they will believe you when you approach them to discuss their shadow behaviours. Unconsciously, they may be a little wary or scared and so become belligerent. Their behaviours could be their defence and protection.

Bullies can be asked to speak to their manager or a coach to address their behaviours. The first step is to be very clear that this is an issue that needs to be dealt with. Consider what will help the person feel comfortable enough to have the discussion. It is worth starting by asking the person about what is positive about them and the skills they have.

You can then begin the discussion about the behaviours. It is best to have a range of examples of their actions and not just opinions. With each example, it is worth exploring what happened, what impact they felt the behaviour had on the recipient, and what they could do differently. Focussing on specifics is more helpful than just saying, 'Let's talk about your bullying attitude.'

If there is sufficient trust and it is necessary, then there could be an exploration of the reasons for their actions. However, it is important to remember that the intervention described above is essentially coaching and supervision, not counselling.

They may not believe you at first and, even if they agree to change and create a plan (stipulating specific behaviours to use) with you, they may revert to type as a test. It is important to keep having the discussions and reinforce the need to change. They may need extra support to do this. It may be helpful for them to have some sessions with an actor/coach who can help them develop a wider range of behaviours to interact with others.

How to cope with being bullied

The first and most important thing to realise is that the behaviours being used by a bully say more about them than you. They speak to the character of the perpetrator and not the survivor. However, because they can make you feel insecure, it is important to remember your strengths and noble qualities. Perhaps have a picture on your phone that reminds you of who you are as opposed to what is being implied.

If you feel powerful enough, consider approaching someone to talk to about these behaviours. They may suggest that you speak to the person and ask them to stop. This will take courage and sometimes it is too much to speak to the perpetrator. If you can speak to them, it will help to rehearse what you want to say with a trusted person. Remember to breathe properly and slowly and to relax. This will help you centre yourself in the discussion. Hopefully this will be successful. If it is not, then think about what else you could do, such as approaching another more senior manager.

If it is not possible to approach anyone, then remember that while you cannot change another's behaviour, you can influence them by how you respond. Practice being quietly assertive, think about different scenarios, and rehearse how you will tackle each one differently. It may take some time for you to establish a more assertive presence consistently.

Fraud and corruption

Fraud

Fraud is defined as 'wrongful or criminal deception intended to result in financial or personal gain' (Oxford English Dictionary). The behaviours, seen in organisations, include bribery, stealing, falsifying documents, extortion, misuse of power and position, and unauthorised use of confidential information. At the individual level, there are many types of fraud, such as being scammed, phishing, and identity theft. Martina Dove's book, *The Psychology of Fraud, Persuasion Scam Techniques*, contains an in-depth analysis of fraud at the individual level.

Why do people commit fraud?

People who are dissatisfied are more likely to commit fraud, especially if they feel that they have not been treated fairly, e.g. being underpaid. Some may be under financial pressure or feel obliged to a superior who has helped them or because it is very much part of the organisational culture. A few commit fraud out of sheer greed. Some can be described as narcissistic and could believe that what they are doing is for the greater good.

The Fraud Diamond provides a good rationale of what can trigger someone to commit fraud. The four necessary elements are: pressure (financial or otherwise); opportunity; rationalisation (sufficient justification); and capability (Wolfe and Hermanson, 2004). If these are all in place and active, then it is highly likely that the person will be fraudulent.

Who could be a victim of fraud?

Fraud can be committed in an organisation that has limited rules and regulations or applies them in a laissez-faire manner. If there are leaders who either tacitly or overtly condone such behaviour, this then gives permission for fraudulent activity.

At the individual level, fraudsters can target people who are seen to be impulsive, have low self-control, are compliant, easily socially influenced, have limited vigilance, and are susceptible to social influence and flattery and intimidation. Dove has devised a very useful model of fraud susceptibility that is worth considering. The model emphasises the need for the right circumstances and fraud offer that then interact with a range of individual characteristics such as compliance and impulsivity; subsequently, the model has strategies for dealing with the offer, including vulnerability.

Survivors of fraud often blame themselves, are angry, probably stressed, and anxious. What seems to matter most is being deceived.

Corruption

This is the 'use of bribery to influence the actions of a public official. Corruption refers to obtaining private gains from public office through bribes, extortion, and embezzlement of public funds' (Oxford English Dictionary).

Individuals holding power are more likely to act corruptly. Having power can lead to over-confidence including in decision making, greater risk acceptance, and a focus on rewards. Overconfidence in their own morality may make individuals less likely to admit or realise that they are acting corruptly.

Those who are powerless may not feel they can stop corruption if they know about it. If they think they will receive rewards, then they are more likely to be tolerant of corruption.

Corruption is more likely when a person stands to gain personally and has lower self-control. They are also likely to think that corruption will only cause indirect harm and, in organisations, is unlikely to be punished. Such individuals are likely to disengage morally and restructure cognitively to justify their behaviours, which will compromise their judgement.

They may also displace responsibility and say that it is the organisation that offers bribes and so it is the organisation that must report the corruption. However, if someone feels guilty, they will be less likely to act corruptly (Anti-Corruption Resource Centre, 2018).

If someone is going to be unethical, then it will be more likely if the external culture supports such actions.

But if the person has a greater locus of self-control and sophisticated cognitive moral development, then they are more likely to make ethical decisions and less likely to comply with unethical management requests.

Reasons

Corruption can mask insecurities. It could start with a need for recognition and resentment or personal gain, financial or otherwise. Being part of a corrupt group can lead to personal recognition. The person could then become loyal to their own values and that of the group. 'You are with us or against us.' They cannot recognise that they could be seen as morally bankrupt.

Corruption can have a detrimental effect on mental health. Sharma et al. (2021) found that experiencing day-to-day petty corruption was associated with psychological distress.

Growing up with such behaviours being seen as acceptable can lead to someone adopting these behaviours. Their continued use will be facilitated by being in an environment that permits their utilisation.

Prevention of fraud and corruption

At the organisational and country level, there need to be clear and well understood policies, procedures, and regulations to discourage fraud and corruption. The culture should be one that promotes openness and honesty and is reflected in the behaviours of all. Ethical behaviours should be encouraged and rewarded. Integrity measures, such as codes of conduct, could also be used. Checks need to be made during recruitment for prior acts and trustworthiness.

It is also important to ensure that the financial and resource use systems are functional, operational, and reviewed regularly, including the production of understandable reports and exception notifications. A system (perhaps anonymous) for staff reporting discrepancies should also be introduced. Ideally, the organisation should also look at its remuneration packages so that staff are paid as they should be and, if so, they will be less likely to steal or become corrupt.

People who commit fraud or are corrupt may be very unlikely to admit having used these actions, even if there is overwhelming evidence. In such cases, the organisation often terminates the person's employment and, sometimes, advises them to seek help to address their issues.

Survivors of fraud or corruption may need help to understand that it was not their fault and that they can be given an opportunity to recover. This also applies to team members of any person who has had their employment terminated, as they will have unresolved feelings.

Wilful blindness, agnotology, and suppression

Wilful blindness

Wilful blindness is a legal term that has been adopted in other sectors. It refers to times when we, as individuals or a group, 'could know, and should know, but don't know because it makes us feel better not to know' (Margaret Heffernan). Her book, Wilful Blindness, describes and analyses many instances in which there was an abundance of wilful blindness which can occur consciously or unconsciously.

A version of it happens, almost automatically, in everyday life, because there is only so much information we can acknowledge and absorb at any one time. Our attention and other cognitive systems have limited capacity. We must manage the wealth of data that comes into us at any one point, and we do this through a variety of mechanisms and filters which are functional but can be skewed in some situations, especially if we are stressed.

We can adopt a blindness, especially if there is information that will challenge or contradict us, our current perspectives, or beliefs. We prefer data that confirms our stance and ignores others. In decision making, this happens quite early in the process.

Factors that contradict our views could be ignored or rationalised away. This happens perhaps because of fear of what would happen if we paid attention to such information. And we may want to keep our power.

Inevitably, these situations will eventually be identified and sometimes in very public ways such as Enron. Heffernan describes how and why this happens very well in her book.

Agnotology

Agnotology studies the act of deliberate and culturally induced ignorance or doubt over existing knowledge or science for benefit by a party. Although it is usually assumed that ignorance is the state of not being knowledgeable or not-yet-knowledgeable, agnotology observes ignorance as a state brought about by individual parties to gain power and profit. People who have backgrounds that promote such actions or are in circumstances that allow them are likely to use these behaviours. Here, the existing scientific knowledge and tools are manipulated and exploited to manufacture misdirection and misinformation.

This is a classic example of the manufacture of ignorance from a corporate organisation. A secret memo of the tobacco industry named *The Smoking and Health Proposal* was revealed to the public in 1979. Authored in the 1960s by the Brown and Williamson tobacco company, the memo revealed multiple tactics that big tobacco companies used to counter 'anti-cigarette forces'. Considering marketing tobacco, the memo states: 'Doubt is our product, since it is the best means of competing with the 'body of fact' that exists in the public's mind. It is also the means of establishing a controversy.'

Tobacco firms spent billions to obscure the facts of health effects from smoking, proactively spreading confusion about whether smoking caused cancer. One such strategy used was to declare that studies linking carcinogens were conducted on mice and such studies did not mean that people were at risk—creating confusion, although it was apparent that smokers experienced many adverse health outcomes.

Interested in the observation that an industry such as Big Tobacco deliberately created confusion regarding scientific knowledge and misled the public to sell a product, a science historian, Robert Proctor, along with a linguist, Iain Boal, coined the neoclassical Greek word for not knowing *agnosis* and termed the study of wilful acts to spread confusion and deceit, usually to sell a product or win favour as 'agnotology'.

Such acts of creating doubt and ignorance have power and are a tool of oppression by the powerful according to Danah Boyd (2019), and this creation of ignorance and doubt is also observed today, e.g. oil companies paying scientists to downplay the effects of climate change.

In the age of social media and the internet, the purposeful manipulation of science to cast doubt and increase ignorance is observed through data void exploitation. Such media manipulators create a world of content online first, and then drive new terminology through the news media, strategically created to achieve epistemological fragmentation or 'unknowledge' or doubtful knowing about subjects in society, e.g. linking anti-vaccine videos to a news clip which was pro-vaccine.

Social media, news, and blogs can be used to only re-confirm one's existing belief system without developing new knowledge, so people remain distracted, especially with repetitive, base entertainment propagating scientific illiteracy, making it easier to spread confusion. Actively partnered with the influence of media, governments, and corporations can encourage cultural ignorance through secrecy, suppression, document destruction, and selective memory.

Agnotology is a reminder that all organisations and workplaces should re-examine ethics, behaviour, and the related impact on the world beyond power and profit.

Ask yourself:

Do I or does my company work towards something that benefits others?
What impact does what I or my company do have on other people?
Are there any negative implications from my behaviour/my company's behaviour?

Suppression

> 'The action of suppressing something such as an activity or publication'
> (Oxford English Dictionary).

Some people will know how to and do suppress their emotions and even their thoughts. This ability can be extremely helpful, especially in the care and humanitarian sectors, as it allows you to work and support people even in very difficult circumstances. However, this skill has its limitations. If it is used all the time, then it is very energy consuming and, eventually, all that has been suppressed is likely to re-emerge as cumulative or chronic stress or other mental health problems.

Knowing how to suppress usually comes from life and work experience. For example, growing up in a household where it was expected or working in an environment such as the armed forces, where it is often assumed that you know how to suppress. Some will recognise they suppress but may not appreciate the extent to which they use this quality.

Suppression, as we mentioned above, takes up a lot of energy. It is best to suppress when needed, with a brief acknowledgement in the moment, and then release what has been suppressed as soon as possible afterwards. 'Oh, my goodness, that was a massive attack on the convoy. Horrible, horrible. Now I need to breathe, inhale, exhale and coordinate the team so that those involved can get the medical and psychological help they need once they enter our compound.' 'Phew, thank goodness, we have established the response, and the team is working hard to stabilise the injured and stay in touch with families. Now I can retreat, rest, and talk about what happened with my partner and my supervisor. I can let go of what I have been holding in.'

How to prevent these factors arising.

Counter wilful blindness and agnotology by working to ensure that there is open and honest internal and external communication in all relationships, and always meet ethical standards. Leaders should share and endorse expectations. Subordinates need to see that those who are more senior are showing adherence to these expectations. The more diverse the workforce, the better.

Similarly, while suppression has its uses, leaders and organisations should also create a culture in which staff can suppress when needed but also get the permission to deal later with the emotionality of the situation, perhaps with professional help. This is especially important for those who work in emergency situations.

Plagiarism

'Plagiarism is presenting someone else's work or ideas as your own, with or without their consent, by incorporating it into your work without full acknowledgement' (Oxford English Dictionary).

With the wealth of information that is available through the internet, it is all too easy to plagiarise. And some do not, but others do. The amount of plagiarism can vary from small amounts to large sections of someone else's original work. There are many famous people who have been accused of plagiarism, including Helen Keller.

On a smaller scale, there is day-to-day plagiarism. Someone in your organisation replicates an old paper under their name; you suggest something in a meeting and then your manager mentions it to his superiors as his idea.

Legislation on plagiarism exists through copyright law and other similar statutes. Some are effective and others less so. For example, it is very difficult to copyright a recipe which, arguably, has led to rampant plagiarism by some famous chefs. In fact, you can play a game with this. If you are watching a famous chef on TV and they show and claim an unusual recipe that is not part of their normal repertoire, google it and sometimes a very similar one appears devised earlier by another less well-known chef.

Why do people plagiarise?

There are, of course, a variety of reasons. First, the person may be lazy and competitive, so they take the easiest route. They may panic or be overwhelmed or not even think it is an issue or that they will be found out. Some may feel that they lack the knowledge, e.g. not being eloquent enough to write in a second language. Plagiarism can ruin a reputation and there may be legal consequences.

Dealing with plagiarism

If a person feels the urge to copy unlawfully, then it is important for them to stop and remember their core values and how they can get the work done honourably. Everyone has ideas and thoughts to contribute. It is worth remembering the guilt that often accompanies plagiarism.

If you think someone is plagiarising, e.g. their written style is very variable, then there are many ways in which you can check. You might use Google and insert one or two key sentences to see what happens. There are, of course, software programmes that will check for plagiarism .

Fear

The American Psychological Association defines fear as 'a basic, intense emotion aroused by the detection of imminent threat, involving an immediate alarm reaction that mobilises the organism by triggering a set of physiological changes.'

Fear is different to anxiety as it is a short-term response whereas anxiety is longer term and future oriented. However, these emotions can be linked, at least for the person who is experiencing them. They both have similar symptoms and whether they indicate anxiety or fear can depend on the label the person and/or others give them. Both can be a component of other mental health issues.

Common symptoms of fear include physical ones such as chest pain, dry mouth, rapid heartbeat, sweating, trembling, shortness of breath, and an upset stomach. There may also be psychological symptoms, such as being upset, feeling out of control, and being overwhelmed.

There can be a degree to which the person experiences fear, and this can vary from trepidation to dread, horror, and terror. Excess fears are commonly known as phobias. These can be triggered by specific stimuli, such as spiders, or can be unspecific.

Fears can also be triggered in the workplace, where there is a close link to anxiety and worry. The triggers include job insecurity, e.g. in a recession or being fearful of a manager or colleague. Fear can then have similar effects to those experienced when under stress, i.e. lowered cognitive performance and less effective thinking, decision making, and attention.

There are several therapeutic techniques for understanding and coping with fears. First, it is important to consider the extent to which your fear is having a negative effect and what are the triggers. It is also important to understand what your fear reaction is from the moment you experience the trigger to the aftermath. You can then see what alternative responses you could use when you experience the trigger. It can help to rehearse the new responses and learn about proper breathing, which can be helpful in calming down.

An alternative approach is known as flooding, where the person is over-exposed to the fear-inducing stimulus. The theory is that flooding, through over-exposure, will lead to a decrease and attenuation of the fear response. This is a very strong approach and can traumatise the person. Its effectiveness has not been completely proven.

Anger

Anger is a normal human emotion which varies from mild to severe. It triggers physical and emotional responses. This emotion drives up heart rate and blood pressure and releases increased levels of adrenaline and cortisol. It is an active emotion—driving us to respond to a situation. It is healthy to feel anger—it can provide us with the motivation we need to act against a wrongdoing or injustice, for example. But anger also risks lowering inhibitions and can make us act inappropriately, aggressively, and even violently. It's important that we learn to control and constructively channel our anger, to protect our own emotional resilience, and to ensure it does not become destructive.

Psychological studies have shown that some people get angry more easily and more intensely than others. Such people have what psychologists refer to as a low tolerance for frustration. They feel they should not have to be subjected to frustration, inconvenience, or annoyance—even if everyone else is. They can't take things in their stride, and they get particularly infuriated if they feel a situation is unjust. Their inability to handle their anger or channel it constructively may affect their personal relationships, their ability to act calmly and professionally at work, and their capacity to navigate the everyday challenges of life like traffic congestion, or inefficient bureaucracy, or the multitude of daily setbacks that make life seem unfair.

To manage anger effectively is not to suppress it. It is healthy to express angry feelings in a calm, assertive, non-confrontational manner. This requires keeping our emotions in control, being respectful of ourselves and others, and articulating clearly what it is we are angry about—without hurting, insulting, or trying to control the response of anyone else.

In contrast, if we do not confront and channel our anger constructively and suppress it instead, it will continue to fester. This can lead to unhealthy responses, including passive-aggressive behaviour, as well as a tendency to cynicism, hostility, and perpetual grumpiness. It can also lead to side effects such as problems with blood pressure or depression.

Anger management aims to reduce both the emotional and physical responses caused by anger. It recognises that while it is not possible to get rid of, or completely avoid, what or who makes us angry, we can tailor our responses.

Some techniques that we can use include:

Rational and logical thinking. When we're angry, we often exaggerate and overly dramatise the situation or problem we're confronting. We can learn to replace these responses with more rational, logical, problem-solving ones. For example, we can persuade ourselves to recognise that while something is deeply frustrating and upsetting, it isn't a disaster, and getting angry won't help resolve the problem.

We can learn to remind ourselves that angry responses alienate or humiliate the people we need to help us get to a solution and will therefore only exacerbate our problem. And we can teach ourselves that as much as we want and insist upon being fair and agreeing—everyone else feels the same, and we're all equally hurt and disappointed when we don't get what we want. We need to learn to ask for and strive for things, rather than demand them as our due.

Problem solving. Sometimes our anger is driven by the feeling of being overwhelmed or helpless in the face of very real and inescapable problems. Occasionally, we can't hope to find a solution right away. But we can learn to face and tackle the problem effectively, and work towards a solution, taking one step at a time, and bringing others along with us.

Calming and controlling outward behaviour and internal responses. Simple relaxation tools, such as deep breathing and visualisation, can be calming. These techniques can be learnt and practiced, so that they can be drawn on automatically in a tense situation.

Thinking before speaking. When angry, our words can escalate the situation, and we will later regret what we have said. Managing our anger requires us to take a moment to think through our responses, pause and then speak. It also necessitates listening to what others are saying and trying to see their point of view. It's natural to feel defensive when we're criticised—but it's much more helpful to listen to the criticism, understand where it's coming from, and respond rationally, rather than leap immediately to aggression and defensiveness.

Using humour. This can remind us not to take ourselves too seriously, get a more balanced perspective, and face our reactions more constructively. Sometimes all it takes is to imagine yourself as an external observer, watching the crazy person (yourself) losing your cool to no avail, to be reminded that anger is more likely to elicit laughter or scorn than sympathy and help.

Take time out. Sometimes we need to give ourselves a break, some personal quiet time, to help us then deal with situations or people more calmly.

Physical activity can help to lower stress levels which can trigger anger. It can also provide an immediate release for angry feelings—if you feel your anger escalating, a slow walk could help to calm you down.

Know your triggers. If you're more likely to get angry in the evening when you're tired, for example, or if a colleague repeatedly presents you with a problem first thing in the morning before you've even reached our desk—you could communicate these triggers to those around you and plan so that problems and difficult conversations take place at more constructive moments in the day.

Pick your battles. If you can, avoid the things that you know will infuriate you. For example, if your daily commute leaves you enraged by the time you reach the office, try to find an alternative route that's less congested or noisy, or leave earlier to miss some of the traffic.

Other toxic behaviours, thoughts, and emotions

Used persistently, these behaviours, thoughts, and emotions (described above and below) can have a very negative and serious impact on the well-being and mental health of individuals and groups. Consistent displays of related actions can lead to toxic work environments, and some may even normalise these behaviours and, perversely, see them as acceptable.

Such environments, especially if their existence is covertly or overtly condoned by leaders and managers, can have adverse impacts on productivity and lead to higher levels of stress and anxiety. Sometimes, employees will seek refuge through the internal justice system which can help but, unfortunately, using them may lead to further problems such as the targeting of whistle-blowers.

As well as the behaviours, thoughts, and emotions outlined above, toxic behaviours include manipulation, cruelty to others, e.g. being invited to and then refused entry to a leaving party, cheating in interviews, and having someone else do your written test.

Toxic behaviours also include those that have been labelled as master suppression techniques and these are aimed at quashing or dominating another. Ingjald Nissen identified nine which were then collated to five and include: making someone feel invisible/silencing/claiming another's work; ridiculing someone; withholding information; double punishment; and blaming or shaming someone.

These actions occur for a variety of reasons, such as resentment, jealousy, competitiveness, and insecurity. Some of these actions are carried out deliberately and others are not.

Interventions

If you have used any of these behaviours, then stop and think about their impact on the receiver and what led you to use them. How would others describe you? Positively or negatively? How can you address these needs more positively, e.g. being competitive or jealous?

If you have been subjected to toxic behaviours, it is important to recognise that such actions say much more about the user than about you. It is important to rethink how you can approach these situations. How assertive were you? What happened and how could you be more assertive next time? How can you detach yourself from these situations? Remember, as David Sheff said, "'I didn't cause it. I can't control it. I can't cure it.' You can, however, manage how you respond.

Review your life and work coping strategies. Perhaps limit how much time you spend with those who use toxic behaviours. Try to establish some boundaries, such as asking them to be polite when speaking to you. They may not believe you at first because, probably, no one else has had the courage to confront them. At times like this, it is important to be as calm and as centred as possible.

None of us can change another's behaviour, but we can control how we respond to them and help to create an atmosphere where the person's negative behaviours will not be accepted. How can you work with others to create a positive work environment in which it will be very difficult for these behaviours to be used? For example, providing feedback for such behaviours, and expecting honesty and openness from all.

The role of emotions

There are many emotions that are linked to both golden and shadow behaviours. Our emotions can facilitate or hinder our being and behaviours. For emotions to be helpful, they need to be positive and in balance with our thinking, decision making, and overall behaviour. If there isn't a balance and/or we choose to let ourselves be driven by the emotion, the outcome can be positive or negative, depending on the situation.

For example, if we feel happy and positive, assess the current issue and situation and decide to act to bring about a positive outcome, then we will be helpful and considerate. However, a negative outcome may ensue if we do not properly assess the situation and, regardless of our positive mood, ride roughshod over someone so that all can benefit.

Sometimes an emotion such as anger can drive us, even at work. This can happen for a variety of reasons, such as there is something that is very irritating in your personal or professional life, like constant arguments, and it is not possible to express fully your anger or any other emotion. Inevitably, these emotions will need an outlet and anger can provide that function. Anger can also be a way of protecting yourself against future (real or imagined) threats. It is important to learn what your triggers and patterns for expressing anger and other emotions are and then learn (perhaps with professional support) healthier ways of expressing your emotions.

On rare occasions, there may be a neurological or physiological reason for the emotion, such as damage to the frontal lobe or limbic system. If this is the case, then we should not expect the behaviour to disappear, even with the most comprehensive of interventions, but we should help the person manage their emotion so that it is within reasonable limits.

Worry can contribute to the expression of either positive or negative behaviours. If we are overwhelmed by worry, then we can become stressed and our cognitive systems also become affected, and this can lead to us using shadow behaviours instead of golden behaviours. A very simple technique for managing this is to breathe slowly and surely, as this will rebalance us. Anxiety can have similar effects.

Our choice of behaviours can also be skewed by 'faulty thinking', and this can happen for a variety of reasons, such as being depressed or having obsessive-compulsive tendencies. These can be addressed with help. For example, if the person keeps thinking and acting negatively, then they can be taught to assess their thoughts and beliefs to look for what is correct and what is not.

How do we become people who focus on the golden or shadow side of life?

Some argue, in developmental psychology and related fields, that people's early background shapes them greatly and that this sense of Self is then further built by subsequent experience and the people who come into our life. There is also often a debate about what has greater impact: nature/genes, or the environment. Even now, with neuroscience, we are no closer to a definitive statement on this issue. There is greater plasticity in us so that we can shape and mould ourselves more than people used to think was possible.

Our backgrounds can explain who we are but do not have to define us. This comes from how (and if) we learn from our history and then how we choose to live.

Siblings from the same family, and therefore from similar backgrounds, can choose very different paths in life. One can select being positive, ethical, and golden and the other can prefer to be the opposite of positivity. This may partly depend on each person's recall of how they were brought up.

Sometimes a person's selection of the shadow side is obvious from a young age. The child who is keen on being selfish to gain more than his siblings could become the ambitious and selfish adult who decides that it is easier to ride roughshod over others.

An adult could select negative shadow behaviours such as harassment because they are insecure in themselves and want to control the situation. They may have only seen negative behaviours being used by managers with whom they have worked and so adopted them.

A person who has grown up with shadow behaviours may have normalised them and find it difficult to behave otherwise. It is also possible that they will find it easier to use these behaviours, especially if they are in a culture that encourages and expects them to do so.

An adult who is secure in their sense of Self (and is ethical) is likely to select behaviours that will enable and permit kindness, consideration, and openness in the teams and people they manage. However, the shadow exists in all of us and sometimes seeks an outlet, and we usually then go against our better natures and then learn from the experience of using them. For example, forgetting to be respectful and saying something nasty to a close colleague and later apologising. On rare occasions, someone will move to the shadow side if they feel that they have been too golden, e.g. being very polite when chairing a very contentious meeting but immediately afterwards lie unnecessarily to a colleague. Being very stressed can close off your positive sense of Self and make you more inclined to move to the shadow side.

An organisation, at its inception, can collectively select to be truly positive and golden or shadow. This is often determined by those who are the leaders. Once the template has been set, this will continue to influence those who then join.

Motown was created by Berry Gordy Junior and produced some of the finest pop music in the 1960s and 1970s. The organisation was eclectic, permissive, and there was a flow of great creativity between artists, writers, and musicians. There was a solid business basis and Motown also ensured that artists were taught about the finer points of etiquette, including social graces. There were, inevitably, some internal issues, such as competitiveness and fairness in pay.

The story of the Chicago Bulls is an excellent example of a collective of leaders, including Michael Jordan and Phil Jackson who, sometimes by coincidence, created a zeitgeist that led to six world championships positively. The Netflix series, *The Last Dance*, is worth watching to see how this happened. It describes the story of the Bulls.

Intriguingly, the qualities that led to the Chicago Bulls' success are probably the same ones that led to the rise of Hitler. Charisma, belief in a common purpose, ability to persuade and influence, and a collection of people who could do the necessary tasks. The biggest difference is the extent to which their goals and actions were moral and ethical for one and all.

Can organisations shift from golden to shadow and vice versa? Yes, and here are some stories. Three organisations, at the start, were extremely value based, democratic, and creative. Employees felt they were part of a greater passion and mission. Each organisation had its faults, e.g. a failure to pay attention to finances or insufficient policies and procedures, but somehow these were not seen as important enough to deter employees from their mission. What seemed to happen was that key people who led the organisation left, or the problem became greater than other issues and then the business went into freefall from golden to shadow.

In the first example, financial problems came to the fore because of fraud and over expenditure. The Chief Executive, rather than asking employees to continuing working for the common goal, instructed them to lie, pretend nothing was wrong, and say to customers that what the press had reported was wrong. This led to some leaving the organisation and disillusion in those who remained.

In the second example, a new Chief Executive started at an organisation that was entrepreneurial with minimal policies and procedures, but still got the tasks achieved in a very ethical and value-based way. She focussed on bringing in structure and process so much that the heart of the work was lost. This was not noticed by the Chief Executive, but those at lower levels saw that suddenly they had to spend inordinate amounts of time filling in paperwork and felt very stifled in their creativity. The work continued, but without heart and true purpose.

The third example is about a leader who was employed (as a political favour) but was not suitably qualified for the post. Hence, this person hired others who also lacked the skills but would dominate and ensure that people with the real expertise were sidelined or encouraged to leave. Even though this section grew, it had the reputation of not really delivering and sometimes being intimidating. However, when the leader left the organisation, a new person was appointed, and they re-assessed the capability and eligibility of each staff member. Those who were eligible remained, and those who did not were supported to find alternatives. The team culture, through hard work, changed and became more positive. There was one exception though: it was decided not to take any action against a staff member (who did not possess the correct qualifications) because of their political connections. The decision was taken to just let their contract expire.

The range of shadow behaviours we have seen in individuals and organisations are so easy to list: malice, fraud, bullying, harassment, mobbing, sabotage, blocking colleagues, and being competitive. If we want to look for reasons for the purpose, use, and maintenance of these behaviours in individuals, then we need to consider the person's background and investigate what is sustaining these actions.

If these behaviours are permitted within an entity, then we need to carry out an organisational analysis to find what has happened, perhaps at the level of leaders and influential groups, and look at what is permissible. Three conditions are necessary for shadow behaviours to be present and used in an organisation: individuals who feel that these behaviours are justified; the giving of permission (sometimes tacitly, through ignoring them and sometimes through fear) for the continued use of them; and the ignoring and/or failure of leadership, appraisal, and internal justice mechanisms to address the negativity.

For example, a serious and sustained example of mobbing was led by three individuals, in different departments, who used their professional knowledge of some junior and senior employees to intimidate and threaten them to mob others whom the threesome disliked. This included reading people's emails, spreading false rumours, sharing confidential information, and blocking or slowing initiatives that the targeted people had been asked to work on. The influence of the three was so strong that many (including leaders) had gotten used to being treated in this way. The whole situation was investigated, finally, and one of the staff, who had been employed for five years, was asked, 'Please tell us why you are still here?' Their response was, 'At least here, I know what they are going to do.' Working in such an atmosphere can dull your senses to what is truly awful. (Later, we provide some suggestions of mechanisms to investigate and then help an organisation shift from shadow to golden.)

How did this situation arise? Two of the ringleaders had started work in the organisation at the same time and were both extremely insecure and jealous of other people's competencies and so, over the years, built up a network of people who had to collaborate to de-stabilise individuals whom the ringleaders felt posed a threat, e.g. being more competent. There was a silent acceptance of their power, which made it difficult to address the matter organisationally until the investigation.

Occasionally, shadow behaviours are serious and contrary to existing internal policies and standards and sometimes the law. Those individuals who commit such acts consistently rarely admit, acknowledge, and own the behaviours. They are more likely to provide, in their eyes, a valid and reasonable rationale for their actions, even in the face of solid photographic evidence.

Shadow behaviours can also occur simply out of ignorance for both individuals and organisations. An apprehensive and inexperienced manager who did not trust her team and who worked remotely, insisted on each person logging on every 20 minutes so she knew they were on their laptops. A Chief Executive, wanting to enhance his organisation's approach to diversity, permitted the use of a poster that was aimed at encouraging diverse people to take part more. This was theoretically a good initiative but, unfortunately, he allowed the use of very negative words to describe different diverse groups. He had been consulted about which words to use and had given the go-ahead in good faith. Inevitably, there were many complaints. The Chief Executive publicly apologised and agreed to consult staff more closely in the future.

All of us (individuals and organisations) should try to understand how we live on the golden or shadow side and keep that balance as much as possible. Having done this, then we can see what impact this has on us, others, and our communities. We are then left to choose to be more golden (or shadow). Let's explore this further.

Some people will find it incredibly easy to work from the golden and maintain a balance, almost keeping the shadow side at bay. The same applies, probably, for those working mainly from the shadow side. In either case, people will maintain that preference and the associated balance. We speculate that if someone is largely golden, they will readily acknowledge if they shift temporarily to the shadow side and rectify matters. Someone who operates from the shadow side may work from the golden sometimes but may be uncomfortable or refuse to acknowledge it or use the golden for their own purposes.

The impact of golden and shadow behaviours on leading

Leading others positively

Leadership has been thoroughly explored, researched, and written about. Some texts look at the individual qualities that are needed, most of which have been explored above. Leadership is something that very few are born with and most learn through experience, modelling others, and being formally taught.

Leadership has been split into different categories by Lewin: autocratic, democratic, and laissez-faire among others, and each has associated behaviours and roles. To lead positively requires the use of inclusive and democratic approaches and knowing when to give orders. An inclusive approach is sufficient and much needed in day-to-day work life. However, in emergencies, it needs to be accompanied by the ability and willingness to give strong instructions while still listening to those who are involved in the emergency response.

The term collective leadership is also helpful to consider as it views leadership as a function in which many can be involved rather than a role carried out by one person. The proper enactment of collective leadership (and similar models such as participatory management and employee-owned firms) often depends on the willingness of all who have been in traditional leadership and more junior roles to be prepared to let go of how they have been operating and to be willing to change to a more collective and collaborative approach.

An inclusive and positive leader will likely focus on using many of the golden behaviours we have articulated above. They will work from a stance of being compassionate, respectful, and work with integrity and professionalism. They will know the shadow behaviours but choose not to use them even when they could. If they inadvertently use such actions, then they are likely to rectify the situation as soon as they realise they have led from the shadow side.

Such leaders usually are very comfortable with their role, who they are and have a great deal of self-trust in themselves. They are trusting of others and delegate from that standpoint. They do not admonish unnecessarily and will do so, if needed, humanly. Their very actions will convey, sometimes without them realising it, their intention as a leader. 'If a staff member died in a country in which we operated, our Chief Executive wanted to be told immediately and be given information and contact details for the family. He would make time to speak to the family and provide them with the help and support they needed. His actions were never publicised, but many knew of them, and that they showed his depth of caring.'

Maintaining a positive leadership stance can take energy, and some will do the utmost to do so by ensuring they are supported formally and informally by others who are like-minded. They will gather information and learn about how to be a more positive leader.

Leading others negatively

Sometimes a person develops a style that shows negative leadership, e.g. being autocratic or too laissez-faire. This is rarely a deliberate choice. They are likely to have learned this by having seen it in action or they may be insecure and unwilling to adopt a deliberative style as this means letting go and allowing others do the work without the leader keeping a very close eye on what is being done.

For some, using an autocratic style means that they feel in control of the situation. Wanting to be in control means that you are likely to use shadow behaviours such as bullying to manage others. Such behaviours can work, but you may not get the best from the people you manage.

Letting go of such behaviours can be extremely hard, especially if the leader has not had the chance or opportunity to develop and use a wider repertoire of leadership styles and behaviours. The first step is to help the person feel secure enough to have the discussion, then support them to learn alternative concepts and behaviours and, crucially, practice them and receive feedback.

Some will use a mix of golden and shadow behaviours as part of their leadership style for many of the reasons we have explained above. However, we suggest that the overall impact on those being led will be negative even if the person uses golden behaviours 90 percent of the time. Just using a shadow behaviour once a month, such as shouting, can lead to a very negative impact that is often threatening and places everyone on alert for that behaviour's recurrence.

People in organisations who are led

Those who work in organisations will also have their own approaches to being golden and/or shadow in their thoughts, behaviours, and emotions. These repertoires will have been built through upbringing, experience, and work histories. It is important to take time to understand their stances and approaches in relation to the golden and shadow continuum so that you can work out how to help, support, and manage.

Summary

Please stop and look at the list you made at the beginning of this chapter. What are your reflections? Now, look at the list below, and write your golden and shadow behaviours, thoughts, and emotions.

GOLDEN	SHADOW
Self-esteem, compassion, kindness, optimism, respect, honesty, transparency, humility, well-being, integrity, diversity and inclusion, communication and building relationships, collaboration, happiness, courage Other behaviours, thoughts, and emotions?	Compassion fade/fatigue, hypocrisy, lying/dishonesty, prejudice and discrimination, hubris, jealousy and envy, pessimism, competitiveness, revenge, psychopathy and sociopathy, Machiavellianism, narcissism, self-sabotage, underperformance, bullying and harassment, fraud and corruption, wilful blindness, agnotology and suppression, plagiarism, fear, anger Other behaviours, thoughts, and emotions?
MINE/OURS	MINE/OURS

Please consider these questions.

What have you learned overall about your use and maintenance of golden and shadow behaviours, thoughts, and emotions? How do you reconcile your use of golden with your utilisation of shadow?

What does your collection of golden and shadow behaviours, thoughts, and emotions say about your sense of Self (individual or collective) and associated role(s)?

What type of leader are you?

Healthy..Unhealthy
(Golden)   (Shadow)

What type of organisation are you?

Healthy..Unhealthy
(Golden)   (Shadow)

Please note down your responses and you can consider them in the next part of the book.

Please pause and reflect on what you have just read.

Section Two

Finding Out

Chapter Three

Readiness And Preparedness For Change

As we have mentioned, neuroscience is teaching us that our minds, emotions, and bodies are more flexible, plastic, and diverse than was thought some years ago. This is splendid news and so it is possible that we can change and shift our individual behaviours, thoughts, and emotions.

We must first acknowledge and recognise that there is a problem to be addressed. This is followed by an acceptance of the need for change and then we can seek ways of getting help. If we are not ready, then we could self-sabotage.

Once we decide (individually or collectively) to change, then we will see that addressing the issues will positively influence ourselves, others, and the greater community. Robert Johnson highlights this very important point in his books. This applies to looking at both golden and shadow aspects.

Change is best attained when we want to both transform and feel secure. Experience tells us it is important to work out how much you really want to change. It may help to talk this through with a trusted person. If it is not the right time or place, then please stop and wait until it feels right for you.

Beyond this point, we present two types of exercises: one for individuals and one for organisations. They merely provide an arena in which you can explore your perspectives. Of course, please add your own questions and mix and match as you want.

For individuals: Am I ready to change?

Please consider these questions. You can do this by yourself or with a good and trusted person. Choose a comfortable place and time in which to explore. Find a way of recording your responses—written or drawn or recorded.

What is the issue that I am concerned about? Try to describe it as practically as possible in terms of emotions, thoughts, or behaviours. (There may be more than one. Please list them and choose one or two that you are willing to explore. Perhaps look at the model (Chapter One) and this may give you some ideas.) An issue could just be that you want to explore your leadership. Then think about these questions.

How is this issue affecting me—positively or negatively, or somewhere in between?

How much is my history having an effect?

What are the golden parts of myself?

What is the balance between the golden and shadow parts of myself? Which side do I prefer? How do I stay on my preferred side?

Where is the issue affecting my life? Use our model (Chapter One) to think about where the issue may lie.

What are the origins of the issue?

What is the impact on my well-being, mental health, and physical health?

How is it affecting my sense of Self and ability to collate and coordinate? What is the impact on my purpose? How easy is it to be open and focus on my future possibilities?

Having answered these questions, stop. Please leave the exercise and do something relaxing. Return to the exercise and summarise the learning in terms of the issue and consider your readiness for change.

- What is the issue and what have you learned?

| |
| |

- How easy or difficult will it be to change?

Very easy ....Too difficult

- How much motivation do you have to address the issue and make alterations?

Not that much..Too much

- How realistic are you being in acknowledging, recognising, and accepting the issue?

Very unrealistic and in denial..Know the reality and accept

- How much courage for change is present?

Very little ....Too much

- How much energy for this change do you possess?

Not enough ....Too much

- How much support do you have for this change?

None..Too much

- What positive/golden aspects of yourself could help?

```



```

- What is the potential for self-sabotage?

None..Massive

Consider your answers and think about whether you are ready to continue the path to change. If so, please carry on with this book. If not, here are some reflections.

Life can be too overwhelming, and so change could be the last thing on your mind. Maintaining the status quo may be about as much as you can do. If it is too much to change, please stop and reflect on this exercise and think about your answers. Perhaps consider how complicated your life is and what you could do to either stay still or move a little. The choice is always yours. If this is not the best moment, then it is time to wait.

Go forward with courage

When you are in doubt, be still, and wait; when doubt no longer

exists for you, then go forward with courage.

So long as mists envelop you, be still;

be still until the sunlight pours through and dispels the mists as it surely will.

Then act with courage.

Ponca Chief White Eagle

My decision is:

Organisational change: Are we ready?

If the intention is to build on the very positive and golden aspects of leadership and culture, then it is likely that you will select from a wide group to do the initial consideration. If the leadership and culture show negativity, then it is usually best to identify one or two trusted people at this point to start this initial exploration. Others can join later. (It may be worth thinking about how to maintain confidentiality of these discussions as a precaution.)

Look at the model and highlight the golden and shadow parts of the organisation for each of the key areas, e.g. we have a respected formal leader but there are some who are working against her.

Identify the key issues that the organisation wants to address and then prioritise.

1.

2.

3.

(Remember that an issue could be that you want to carry out a general exploration to find out more about the organisation as it is today. If you select this option, some questions below may not be suitable.)

Please consider the questions below for each of the prioritised issues.

How is the issue affecting the organisation?

What is the balance between the golden and shadow parts? Which is more preferred and how is it maintained?

What are the sources of well-being, mental health, and physical health?

How is the issue affecting the ability of the organisation to achieve its purpose and mission?

To what extent is the organisation's history having an effect?

How facilitative is the organisational culture and leadership (formal and informal)?

What are the origins of the issue? Have a look at our model (Chapter One), please, for ideas.

To what extent is the Organisational Self (and ways in which roles are enacted) known, recognised and influential? How much does the Self coordinate what happens? How is the overall health of individuals and groups in the organisation? How open are they to the future?

Please summarise your findings here.

Then answer the questions below.

If change is selected, then how easy or difficult will it be to change?

Very easy ....Too difficult

How much motivation is present?

Not that much...Too much

How realistic is the formal leadership in acknowledging, recognising, and accepting the issue?

Very unrealistic and in denial..Knows the reality, accepts, and truly wants to change

How realistic is the informal leadership in acknowledging, recognising, and accepting the issue?

Very unrealistic and in denial..Knows the reality, accepts, and truly wants to change

What is the balance between the golden and shadow parts of the leadership and organisation?

Very unbalanced..Absolute harmony

How realistic are the staff and other stakeholders in acknowledging, recognising, and accepting the issue?

Very unrealistic and in denial..Know the reality, accept, and truly want to change

How much courage for change is present?

Very little ....Too much

How much energy for this change is available?

Not enough ....Too much

How much support is there for this change?

None ....Too much

What is the potential for sabotage?

None...A massive amount

Consider your answers and reflect on whether this is the right time. Hopefully it is, so please move on to the next chapter.

Sometimes it is best to wait. A Chief Executive wanted to wait four years to announce and implement a national strategy, which is a long time. He explained his rationale—he wanted to delay until the political situation was conducive to have the plan accepted, resourced properly and then implemented. He did this; the strategy was accepted and there were no major hiccups. It was likely that the strategy would have failed or not been accepted if he had tried to implement it quickly.

If it is not the time to bring about large-scale change, then what can be done to make the situation more positive for the staff?

Our decision is...

Chapter Four

A Deeper Assessment

It is time to take, as Otto Scharmer says, a dive at the individual and/or organisational level. It is best to do this in the company of others whom you trust, who really, really know you, can give you good, honest reflections and feedback, and do not have a shadow agenda such as wanting to belittle you or the organisation.

There are two sets of questions: for individuals and then for organisations. Please mix and match.

You can, of course, use your own set of questions. If you do, please stop, and think about whether you have selected the ones that will lead your farther on your journey courageously. Alternatively, if the selected questions are as much as you can cope with, that is also fine.

Caveats

We are all recovering from having lived through the pandemic and all the restrictions. And this has had an impact on our mental health, so it is important to explore in a way that is comfortable for you.

There are choices here, focussing on the golden alone or just the shadow or both. Too much golden can blur our perspectives and we can become complacent. Too much shadow may mean that we have forgotten about what could be golden and that decency is the norm.

Selecting to only look at one aspect may be helpful, but it is unlikely to lead to a realistic and honest assessment. It may be a sign that you may not want to change what is required but want to maintain the status quo.

Ideally, we should give ourselves permission to consider both the golden and shadow aspects. However, usually, we are not used to in-depth reviews and so may be cautious. What can you do to help yourself or others be ready for the exploration?

If you are an individual and are thinking about exploring your shadow and golden side, then please consider what is needed to help you open yourself to this possibility. Perhaps begin by exploring what is golden about you and praise yourself for being golden and using associated behaviours. You could then select one shadow aspect or behaviour to explore, starting with thinking about a time when you used it and then just reflect on the situation and note what comes through as feelings. It could help to set the scene by making sure that you are relaxed and at a time and place where you can be reflective. Having someone you know and trust alongside can also help.

Choosing to build on just the golden aspects can be good and worthwhile. If this is the option you select, it is vital that you are honest and realistic with yourself and take a few moments to consider the shadow side so that you at least maintain harmony between golden and shadow.

It will take time to persuade colleagues in an organisation that it is worth looking at the golden and shadow sides. They will need and want reassurance that they can speak freely without repercussions.

If shadow thoughts, emotions, and behaviours are being utilised in an organisation, then it is vital to consider how these are brought into the open. If this is done in a way that makes people insecure, then they are likely to sabotage your efforts. Consider how you can help people feel comfortable and think about other healthier ways in which they can interact in the organisation. We suggest that the first step is to consider how you can build more openness and willingness to have such discussions. A way to start this process is by the leaders showing that they would like more openness and then disclosing something to show that intention. This is likely to help people know you are serious. This action needs to be followed up by other similar behaviours. Hopefully, trust then builds, and this should eventually facilitate conversations about the golden and shadow.

At all times, it is important to only disclose what you want not what you think others may expect. This also applies if you are helping someone explore their shadow and golden side either as an individual or in groups.

Above all, we hope you choose to consider, in tandem, the golden and shadow aspects so that you can carry out a real exploration of what is going on.

The exploration using the models

In this section, we provide you with exercises and questions to continue your journey of exploration, both as a person or as a larger group.

An assessment for individuals

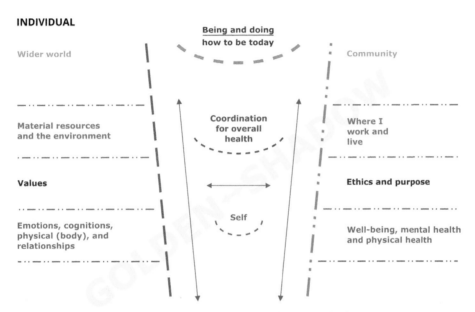

INDIVIDUAL

Wider world

Being and doing
how to be today

Community

Material resources
and the environment

Coordination
for overall
health

Where I
work and
live

Values

Ethics and purpose

Emotions, cognitions,
physical (body), and
relationships

Self

Well-being, mental health
and physical health

Personal history and community history (known and unknown)

Make an appointment with yourself to do this exploration. Choose a time and place where you know you can feel comfortable and yet ready to explore. Allocate at least half a day. It may help to identify someone to help you on this journey.

Make sure that you take breaks and have snacks and foods available. As the Dalai Lama says, food and drink help the flow of meetings and sustain those present.

Having selected the time, place, and supports, here are some ways in which you can prepare for the exploration. Think about how you will record your deliberations and findings to consider at the exploration.

> For about a week, make some time at the end of each day to reflect on which types of emotions, thoughts, and behaviours you have used and why. What influenced you? What is the purpose of your golden and shadow sides? What is the balance between golden and shadow? Which elements have protective qualities? What role does your history have in your current day-to-day life? How much did you stop, pause and consider the future?

Have a look at the elements of the model to see which aspects were present/shaped your day. How did the golden and shadow link to your sense of Self and the role you have?

Carry out a detailed global assessment and consider each of the key areas.

Who/what is part of your wider world and community? How do they influence you now?

What is the effect of the available material resources and the environment?

Where do you live? Where do you work? What is the impact of where you live and work?

What words would you use to describe your values/ethics and sense of purpose? How do they give meaning to your life?

What is the impact of your history on your current life and approaches?

How is your physical health? How is your mental health and overall well-being? What adjustments do you need to make daily because of your overall health?

Describe your known emotions and cognitions (how you think, listen, pay attention, decide, remember, and recall). Who is in your work life? What do they say about your leadership style? To what extent do your leadership style and relationships reflect the golden side versus the shadow side?

What do you know about the people you manage, their roles and use of golden and shadow behaviours? What is your evidence? How does this influence how you work with them?

What are your golden and shadow behaviours, thoughts, and feelings? What, for you, is the purpose and function of the golden and the shadow? Which ones protect you? Which ones are hindrances? What other parts of yourself are connected to the golden and shadow, e.g. values, emotions, memories? Which act as triggers? Which ones maintain the golden or the shadow?

How harmonious is the balance between golden and shadow? What reinforces and maintains the current balance between golden and shadow?

How would you describe your sense of Self? What is the image that comes to mind? What/who influences your Self and life coordination? What is your alignment with purpose, promotion of physical and mental health, quality of physical environment, and abundance of material goods, including salary? How important is global sustainability to you? How much time do you give to reflecting about the future?

What is the connection between your Self, your formal role, and the golden and shadow?

What helps you coordinate your sense of Self? For example, what is uppermost, e.g. the need to maintain your values or to please your manager? Which aspects of your personal life are positive and helpful? What/who could steer you towards negativity? What/who helps you remain golden?

Write a list of behaviours, thoughts, and emotions that you have showed at work and place them along this continuum

Golden .... Neutral .... Shadow

Consider your findings and explore the reasons you have located yourself as you have. Which behaviour is used most frequently and why? What is the known and unknown history and reason for this repertoire? How have they helped/hindered you? What is the connection with your Self?

Make a list of one or two people you have disliked/been uncomfortable with. Write their characteristics (positive and negative). To what extent do they reflect your golden and shadow side? What is the learning point?

Think back to your last month. Which behaviours, emotions, and thoughts along the golden-shadow continuum did you use? What activated them? Now, think about how you felt about your sense of Self and how much you were ethical when you carried out those behaviours.

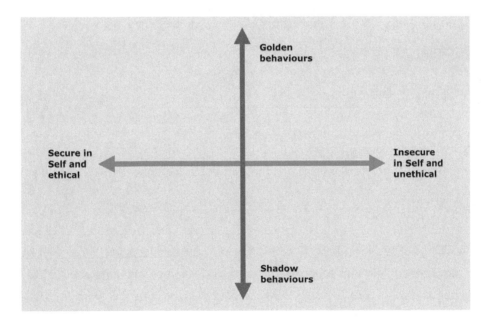

Please populate the diagram with your findings. What have you learned about yourself?

For example, when Vondra did this exercise, she realised she was more likely to use shadow behaviours when she was tired, lacked confidence, and felt blurry about being ethical. 'I am more likely to lie when I am tired and when I am in the company of those who lack candour. I also realised that I have standards below which I will not go in terms of behaviours and ethics. I have, when I worked in organisations, been asked to condone harassment because of the power and seniority of the person and because the usual internal justice systems were unlikely to address the behaviours owing to the power of the person who harassed. On these occasions, I could have been silent but sometimes chose instead to circumvent the internal justice system and speak informally to more senior people to ask for their help to resolve the situation. Admittedly, sometimes I could have said or done more but was afraid to because of the consequences I could face.'

Create a scene in which three characters are going to have a discussion: Self, Shadow, and Golden. Imagine them having a discussion or you could do this with trusted people, via role play, with someone observing.

You could also ask the characters these questions:

How did you come into being? What is your name? How is your existence maintained?

What are the links between the three of you?

Which of you helps and hinders Self?

Create a sculpture of your golden and shadow parts and Self (including your role). Leave it in a place where you can see it and reflect on the feelings that are generated. Having done so, what would you like to keep or remove?

Think about who is in your life. Include both formal and informal relationships. Who is in your inner circle and who is in your outer circle? Who supports you, and who is critical and judgemental? What reinforces the positive and negative aspects of yourself? How has your history influenced who is in your life?

What is in your life? How do each of these aspects reflect and reinforce the golden and shadow sides?

On a piece of paper, draw three concentric circles. Write your initials in the centre. Think about who is most and least relevant in your life. Select symbols for each group, e.g. people you are close to (triangle), people who are acquaintances (square), and locate them in one of the circles. People who are very close to you should be in the inner circle.

Think about the nature of each relationship. If it is positive, then draw a straight line between your initials and the person. If, however, the relationship is negative, then draw a broken line.

What have you learned about these relationships and their golden and shadow aspects?

Explore your emotions and think about the extent to which you release or suppress them. What are your reasons (both historical and present day)? What would happen if you stopped releasing and/or suppressing them?

Write a letter congratulating yourself on having coped with life now and in the past. What would you like to praise yourself about?

Make a list of positive adjectives that others would use to describe you.

Ask others to write to you about how you are with them. What is positive? What could change to improve the relationship(s)?

Think of four words that describe your behaviours that you like and appreciate. Write them on a piece of blank paper, then draw an image that depicts, to you, their meaning and significance.

Turn the paper over and select four words that describe behaviours you do not like or appreciate. Again, please write them down or draw an image that outlines, to you, their significance and meaning.

Fold the paper into a circle with the side of behaviours you like on the outside. Secure the fold, then reflect on what you have drawn or written either by yourself or with others.

Golden building blocks

Think of your life and select those people who have helped to shape you positively and who continue to do so. Make a note of how they have influenced you in the past and currently.

For example, Anna's great-grandfather was a respected priest in the north of Sri Lanka. He died in 1921 and is still remembered for his work, as is his wife. Although she did not know them, they are very much an influence on how she tries to be.

Reverend Samuel Eliatamby

'In any estimate of human stature, he ranked high, alike in physique as in the impact he made on the varied activities of the parish' (Description about Reverend Eliatamby from a history of the church(Glimpses)).

Mary P. Eliatamby (Inscription on her plaque in Uduvil Church, probably written by Reverend Eliatamby):

'By instinct of a spirit true, noble, loving, silent, gentle; she had peace and strength. She stood beautiful before God and in concord with all men.'

The place of compassion and kindness in your life

These qualities are so easily forgotten and yet they are so central to us if we are to be seen as those on the healthy side of life as individuals or organisations.

Please choose a picture that depicts compassion and kindness to you. Reflect, when calm, on the picture and think about how much being compassionate is present in your daily life, practice, and habits. How is compassion present for your Self and others? How much time do you allow for pause and reflection? To what extent does your present personal and work environment allow compassion? If it does not, how do you manage?

What have you learned?

You could use this table as a guide to summarise your reflections

Area	Comments
My golden and shadow side	
Interacting with the wider world and community	

Material resources and the environment	
Where I work and live	
My values, ethics, and purpose	
My emotions, cognitions, physical (body), and relationships	
My well-being, mental health, and physical health	
My history	
Anything else?	

Based on your reflections and how you have completed the table, what have you learned about your Self, its coordination, openness to the future and role in your overall health?

My sense of Self	

Stop and reflect on what your answers have said about what you know about yourself. What therefore is/ could be unknown?

Now please go back to the issue at hand (if you have highlighted one) in the light of what you have learned. What have you realised about the issue, its reasons for being, and its presence in your life? What is golden and what is shadow about the issue? Which golden aspects could help to address the issue?

Based on the above, please answer these questions (we asked the first one earlier in Chapter Two).

What type of leader are you?

Healthy...Unhealthy
(Golden)   (Shadow)

Think of significant people in your life. What would they say about your conclusions? Imagine explaining your data and findings to a stranger or wise person. What would they say?

Organisational assessments

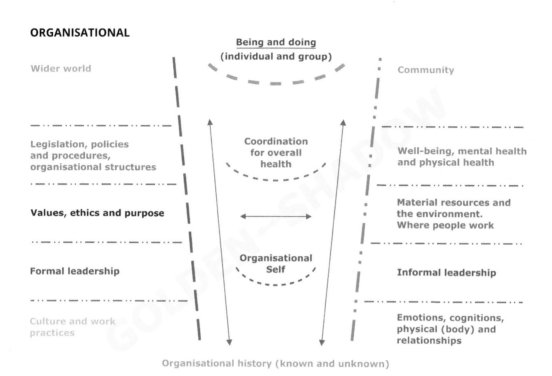

ORGANISATIONAL

Being and doing
(individual and group)

Wider world

Community

Legislation, policies
and procedures,
organisational structures

Coordination
for overall
health

Well-being, mental health
and physical health

Values, ethics and purpose

Material resources and
the environment.
Where people work

Formal leadership

Organisational
Self

Informal leadership

Culture and work
practices

Emotions, cognitions,
physical (body) and
relationships

Organisational history (known and unknown)

This may take much longer than an individual self-assessment, simply because the scope and arena are larger.

There are many methods for organisational assessments when looking at the psychological health of an organisation. It is best to create a small group who represents the organisation, from the very senior to the most junior, to select how this assessment can be done inclusively.

You may want to include quantitative data such as sick leave, numbers of staff who needed to be performance managed, numbers of complaints about bullying and harassment, usage of internal justice systems, surveys on staff views, well-being, etc. The British Standards Institute and MIND have assessment processes to look at well-being (physical and mental health), others look at occupational health and safety. While none of these specifically compare golden and shadow aspects, they can provide valuable data.

Others may adopt a more qualitative approach (such as a large-scale event at which sufficient representatives of the different layers of the organisation come together to look at the model) and provide their views and reflections so that they can collectively develop a perspective from which to act. Some of the individual exercises described above could be adapted for use with large groups.

We recommend you choose a method that is inclusive and reflective of your aim and purpose for the change to follow. For example, if you want to encourage openness, then the assessment process must reflect that.

If the level of trust is very low, then employees are unlikely to take part willingly and may not attend events or take part in surveys. What can you do to show that you really want to consider the issues and deliver change? Perhaps you can be honest about what is shadow and acknowledge it publicly. Remember to mention golden aspects. While some may disbelieve your intent, others may give you a chance. What is certain is that you must show authenticity after your public statement by what you say and do.

Two very helpful and inclusive methods are Building Community Resilience and Asset Based Community Development (John McKnight), both of which can be adapted for organisations. A combination of these can start with the community of concern defining its vision, then creating questions and processes to investigate the current situation against the vision followed by the development of a community map of assets and areas for growth and then a plan for change based on the map.

Here are some key questions to consider.

What are the issues/behaviours of concern that need to be addressed?

What is known about the organisational history? What has been assumed about the growth of the organisation? How has the past influenced the present?

What words would you use to describe the organisational culture? Who keeps it alive? What groups and cliques exist (formal and informal) to maintain the culture?

To what extent is there alignment with purpose, promotion of well-being, mental health, and physical health?

What are the stated values, ethics, and purpose? How much do they steer the behaviours in the organisation? How much does the purpose fit the world of today? Who believes and enacts the values, ethics, and purpose? Who does not and why?

What is the quality of the physical environment and abundance of material goods, including salary?

How much does the physical environment promote and facilitate golden behaviour as opposed to shadow actions?

In terms of the legislation, policies, processes, and organisational structures, how much do they reflect and promote the golden positive side, e.g. the use of compassion, and how much do they focus on the shadow and negative?

(For example, most human resources policies concentrate on actions to take if there are aberrant behaviours. Of course, some do also describe codes of conduct, but there is usually very little about how to promote and support compassion in staff, either by themselves or through management and leadership practice. We have yet to see a procedure that describes the need to be respectful, kind, honest, compassionate, and inclusive in such a way that employees understand what to do differently.)

How responsible is the organisation to the wider world and community? Positively or negatively responsible? How much influence does the wider world and community have on the organisation and vice versa? How important is the global need for sustainability? What is done towards sustainability?

What is the accepted list of golden and shadow behaviours and associated work practices? How are they activated? Who promotes them, and who blocks or tries to stop them? What is their function? What do they help with and what do they prevent?

What other parts of the organisation are connected to the golden and shadow, e.g. values, memories? Which act as triggers? Which ones maintain the golden or the shadow?

Who are the formal leaders and informal leaders? Who has the most power and influence? To what extent is each set working on the golden and/or shadow side?

What is the quality of relationships that are present, both formal and informal? How supportive are they?

Which emotions are permissible? Which ones are not?

What are the prevalent styles of thinking and decision-making? How helpful are they?

How would you describe the collective Organisational Self? Who/what keeps coordinates and maintains it? For example, is there an informal dress code and behaviours that are seen as acceptable or unacceptable?

How flexible are the staff in the organisation? How open are they to the new and unexpected?

What is the overall health of the staff? What factors impede overall health and which ones facilitate it?

What is the connection between the Organisational Self and the golden and shadow?

What has been learned?

You could use this table as a guide to note down your key findings.

Key area	Comments
Use of golden and shadow behaviours	
Formal and informal leadership	
Culture and work practices	
Values, ethics, and purpose	
Physical environment and material goods	
Where people work	
Well-being, mental health, and physical health	
Wider world and community	
Legislation, policies, procedures, and organisational structures	
Emotions, cognitions, physical (body), and relationships	
Organisational history	
Anything else?	

Based on the above, what have you learned about the Organisational Self, coordination, openness to the future, its role in overall health and associated leadership?

Organisational Self	

Therefore, what type of organisation are you?

Healthy...Unhealthy

(Golden)   (Shadow)

Once all the data has been gathered, take time to analyse and cross check the findings. You could present them to a wide group of stakeholders who can then look at the results, validate them, and use them to think about the future.

It can help to ask members of the group to adopt roles (temporarily) and look at the findings from both the golden and the shadow perspective.

You could also produce a report using the key areas to structure it and that is your prerogative. It is your choice.

An alternative would be to create a podcast with all involved. People could then listen to the podcast in a room with art material, including paper, and then record their reactions, responses, and learning. You could then collate what has been written or drawn as a huge collage and simply look at it and reflect. When you feel ready, discuss and summarise the major learning points.

Finally, make sure that you ask: 'Now that I/we have looked at the known, what is the unknown that I/we need to uncover and address?' Please remember to consider the golden as well as the shadow and the counterpoints.

Please, stop and focus on the picture and what you have learned. What image of your future comes to mind?

Section Three

Where Next?

Chapter Five

What is the reason for this chapter? Because we have learned that there are always many perspectives on each issue and that we can only advance if we listen to others. Each of the experts here provides a different view on healthy leadership and healthy organisations.

We interviewed some so that they could share their ideas and others wrote their own section.

Diversity, inclusion, and leadership—two separate views from David Bryan and Sonia Watson

Understanding privilege—Emmicki Roos

Human resources perspectives for healthy leadership—Michael Emery

Agent of change—Richard Beckhard with eulogy from Greg Parston

Changing habits, cognitively and practically—Jamie Ripman

Cooperation and collaboration—Johan Schaar

Their perspectives may help you to reflect more and think about positive solutions.

Diversity, inclusion, and leadership
Sonia Watson

Sonia has a fascinating background, perspective, and expertise in diversity which began when working in the banking industry. Her honesty, humanity, grace, and expertise are shared with us below, starting with an account of her background.

Background and learning about diversity and leadership

Sonia is the daughter of Jamaican immigrants who grew up in Northampton in the Midlands (England). Her parents shared their views of the world in which she and her siblings would grow up. Education and the need to work twice as hard to advance were cornerstones of her upbringing. They also reminded her that diverse people did not really feature in most hierarchies.

She moved into banking and became one of the most senior executives from a non-white background in a UK bank (with a global presence). There were other diverse staff at lower levels, but not in leadership positions. She was not entirely comfortable in her senior role as it was not something she had expected. She realised that her promotion was an exception, and that there were others, perhaps more talented, who had not been given the same opportunities. As she adjusted and remembered her mother's words, 'whatever power you're given, use it for good', she realised she could make a difference by helping others be promoted. She led an initiative to recruit and promote people through merit as opposed to nepotism. Her own confidence and self-belief kept growing. (Interestingly, she opted not to be part of a black support network as she considered they were largely focused as fora for discussion.)

Years later, particularly after the inauguration of President Obama in 2009, she realised that much more was possible. Leadership from diverse people could come from anywhere. It was a vital and pivotal moment for Sonia. She realised she could do more to dispel any myths that diverse people from minority races could not be leaders, especially if they came from particular backgrounds. She became more comfortable being the only diverse person, in terms of race, in the room and being seen as the representative spokesperson for many.

A key facet of Sonia's leadership qualities is in the operationalisation of allyship. This has helped her, in the past and currently, to continue to enable and facilitate others, especially as the diversity agenda widened from gender to race to other differences such as LGBTIQ+. Leaders ought to ask themselves what they are doing to facilitate diversity. Are people from a very wide range of backgrounds being given every viable opportunity to be recruited and stay?

The murder of George Floyd was tragic, but it opened a global discussion for diversity in so many ways. Some leaders paused and reflected on what they had done so far.

Sonia's leadership has grown and continues to do so. She is much more prepared and comfortable being seen in her role within the field of diversity. She will not shy away from what she can do. Sonia may be one, but she knows there are 'ten thousand' behind her who have, through their own adversity, paved the way and facilitated her journey. This poem underpins her current approach.

> 'I am only one, but still I am one, I cannot do everything but still I can do something; and because I cannot do everything, I will not refuse to do something I can do.'
> —*Edward Everett Hale*

Sometimes, if you are from a minority community and in leadership, you are expected to prove that you are worthy of the post. Those from privileged backgrounds often just assume that they are deserving of their positions, even if they lack the capabilities. Occasionally, some have questioned Sonia's presence in a meeting, for example, refusing to shake her hand (something that occurred in 2004). At such moments, she remembers what Oprah Winfrey said—that diverse people deserve to be present, and that she (Sonia) has ten thousand people supporting her metaphorically. This helps, especially because such actions are disconcerting.

Diverse leaders rarely face overt discrimination these days. It is more likely to be covert. However, it is so vital to remember that any discrimination has a stressful impact on the receiver.

Leadership qualities for diversity and inclusion

Senior leaders carry the responsibility for the culture and the organisation. This is often a heavy obligation. Transparency, openness, and being willing to admit fault are key. For there to be progress around diversity, it is necessary to acknowledge what has been lost because of the past failure to be truly inclusive; that such leaders could have been much more successful had they been willing to understand and accept the power of diversity and inclusion. Once leaders are willing to acknowledge this, then they can alter the values of the leadership team to become more inclusive and put in place a change management process that will filter through the organisation with continued involvement from the leadership. 'It needs to start at the top and stay there.'

Diversity and inclusion must be embedded in all aspects of an organisation—policy, processes, clients, and suppliers. There also ought to be meaningful chances for people's voices to be heard and included in transforming the prevailing culture.

Healthily addressing the negative aspects of an organisation

This should start with the leadership and organisation being willing to open up their behaviour and culture so that people feel they can ask questions about everything. Encouraging people to be more open and value transparency will enable leaders and staff to ask questions about the negative aspects and how to address them. A more accessible atmosphere will give permission to diverse staff, who may already be in the organisation, to speak up and have their voice heard (and not repeatedly with the same message that there needs to be change!), secure in the knowledge that sharing their experiences will lead to meaningful change.

Leaders need to acknowledge and accept that affinity biases exist and are operationalised daily in some organisations and throughout wider society. Some look for others like themselves when recruiting, e.g. whether the person plays golf, or is from a similar race or educational background. Affinity bias flows through everything and is possibly the biggest battle to be had for diversity so that leaders can come from anywhere.

Leaders also need to admit that there will be times when they simply don't know. Being willing to be more questioning requires a good amount of self-comfort with yourself so that it is OK to admit that you, as a leader, will not always know the answer. It is imperative to keep asking why? Why? Why? And be ready to learn and keep absorbing.

Why have we not recruited more diverse people? Perhaps some of our expectations exclude them? For example, an organisation required that applicants be fluent in two languages. However, those from some educational backgrounds may not have been able to learn a second language. On trying to understand why a second language was an essential qualification, it became clear that successful candidates could be offered the opportunity to master a second language relatively quickly once in post. Changing this requirement meant that more diverse candidates felt confident to apply.

Other questions to ask include these: What don't we know about diversity and inclusion? What have we done to ensure that our aspirations and plans for diversity are properly embedded? How can we include diverse voices so that their input translates into tangible actions?

We need to accept that some may have had greater opportunities and grown up with privilege, so what can we all do to look around and help someone access the same chances that we have had? How can you help that person on their journey? Perhaps by taking a step back to reflect on your own path? The then Chief Executive of the bank, on his arrival, asked to meet Sonia regularly because he wanted to understand why she was the only diverse person in the room. They met regularly, and he supported her in her career with understanding and compassion. He even explained why it would better for her not to just focus on diversity and equalities but on mergers and acquisitions as it would take her farther in society and lead to greater respect. Through discussions with Sonia, he expanded his perspectives on diversity.

Leaders and organisations need to move beyond perceived 'quotas', which are deemed unlawful, to measurable targets (in line with other organisational goals) that are workable, challenging, and can succeed. Crucially, progress (or not) needs to be reviewed and investigated by continually asking questions. Why? Why? All diversity initiatives need to start with a good review of what has been done to implement diversity to date. This will provide a solid basis for target setting. A website that encourages selling of personal items found, on doing research, that they were not being used by people from diverse communities to advertise items for sale. This was a great surprise to them, and they then found better ways of encouraging people from all backgrounds.

Training has its place, but it needs to continue beyond the classroom. Attitudinal shifts need to be followed by changes in behaviour. Teaching staff about unconscious bias has its limitations, as Sonia says, 'Why are you spending valuable time in a workshop, learning about something you already know exists?'

It is important to still have energy for the work as Sonia does. 'I am not tired of this quest. Many of us are not. There is a window of opportunity, we need to make sure it becomes an open door and then an open room, leading to an open society where everyone has the opportunity to contribute and succeed.'

A hope for the future

This, for Sonia, lies in the phrase 'Blueprint for all'. It is the name of the organisation for which she works, and it is also a phrase used by Dr Martin Luther King.

'Number one in your life's blueprint should be a deep belief in
your own dignity, your own worth, and your own somebodiness.

'Don't allow anybody to make you feel that you are nobody.
Always feel that you count. Always feel that you have worth.
And always feel that your life has ultimate significance.

'Secondly, in your life's blueprint, you must have, as a basic
principle, the determination to achieve excellence in your various
fields of endeavour.

'And finally, and finally, in your life's blueprint, must be a commitment to the eternal principles of beauty, love, and justice. However young you are, you have a responsibility to seek to make your nation a better nation in which to live. You have a responsibility to seek to make life better for everybody. And so you must be involved in the struggle for freedom and justice.'

—*Dr Martin Luther King*

Diversity, inclusion, and leadership
David Bryan

David has worked in diversity, equity, and inclusion for many years and possesses a wealth of experience from which we can learn. He has a solid background in enhancing diverse perspectives in education, arts, and communities which began when he was at school. He has had a substantial influence on the arts in the United Kingdom (UK) and is currently the Chair of Battersea Arts Centre, Brixton House Theatre, and Creative Lives (UK). He was awarded the CBE in 2021 for his contribution to the arts. David has also worked with the leadership of numerous organisations to help them consider their current approach to difference, undertake changes, and work towards greater equity.

David's background

David was born in London, England, of Jamaican working-class parents. He went to a school where 40 percent of the pupils were black, and this contributed to them feeling that they were not a minority, which led to the students being confident and feeling that they had a significant presence. Sixth form pupils set up a Black Debating Society with the school's permission, and this was very popular at the school and others nearby. Often 200-300 would attend the events and speakers included historians (black history), politicians, and civil rights activists. (The Civil Rights Movement in USA was at its height.) The pupils also had access to literature that was not part of the traditional curriculum, e.g. Europe's role in Africa, de-schooling society.

The more he learned independently, the more he came to the view that the curriculum of the time was not valid as it did not adequately include diverse perspectives, especially in history and literature. Several black pupils (including David) found their voices through their independent learning and felt compelled to act, challenging teachers and organising demonstrations against police action towards black people and many other issues. 'We knew that there were alternative views of the world.'

This was the beginning of David's introduction to diversity and social injustice. He then decided to leave school at the age of 15 as he felt it was a waste of time and space, especially because he wanted to change society. He left home and became a squatter, also in Brixton. He was among those who also questioned the status quo and wanted opportunities for diverse voices to be heard. This included Olive Morris who was a local leader and champion for equality and justice. A magazine called *The Black Liberator* was produced in Brixton to reflect black intellectual thinking.

One of the groups he joined wanted to counter the lack of knowledge and ignorance in curricula about diversity; they created and opened their own bookshop in Brixton using their own limited funds. They believed in the power of knowledge and wanted real education to be liberating. The bookshop was very successful, moved to the centre of Brixton, and became pivotal as a black social enterprise with political perspectives. They began the bookshop with zero knowledge about the book trade and enterprise. The collective was driven and staged the first ever Black Book Fair in the UK. 'And we learned by doing.' He wanted to make a change and encourage others to do so as well in all aspects of their lives.

Later, the UK economy went into decline and there were events such as the three-day week and increased discrimination towards black people, e.g. in society and mainstream organisations. David had no formal qualifications but worked with collectives, debating, sharing, learning, and trying to create solutions for change. He also learned by being involved in participatory organisations that wanted transformation through collective effort, And he learned to determine strategy, work to strengths, and decide outcomes.

He left the bookshop to expand his horizons and became the director of St. Matthew's Meeting Place (SMMT), a church-based community centre in Brixton, through the support of Reverend Bob Nind who wanted the church to have a larger role in the local community and become a haven. Given the limited opportunities for community-led activities, their community arts initiatives increased and thereby gave a platform to black creatives who wanted to have their voices heard. David renamed SMMT as Brixton Village and they produced a wide range of theatre productions, black film festivals, mime, and comedy in 1976. They filled a void during a time when black culture and arts were not given a platform; more importantly, they enabled black communities to create their own stories. All this sterling work was conducted at a time when there was considerable overt discrimination publicly in recruitment and employment. Some of this was brought to the public eye through the Scarman report.

David used his immersion in community to move into education, still with no qualifications. He taught on a variety of programmes to facilitate access to education for black people, and he became an advisor to two universities and was an Examiner at Southbank University. He then decided to study for a postgraduate qualification (MBA), as it offered him the opportunity to affirm his managerial and learning experience. This would be his first formal qualification.

His leadership style evolved into one where you look for bigger change, build constituencies, affirm your own independent voice, and don't follow trends of either the right or left wing. Based on his unique experience of leadership and cultural diversity, he was commissioned by the Arts Council of England to undertake several organisational reviews of culturally diverse projects. Following a review on dance, he decided that the black dance fraternity was not being given the same opportunities as white dance communities. He was determined to break the pattern and any misunderstanding that this was how things had to be. He persuaded the Southbank Centre (a premier arts venue) in London to produce a three-day black contemporary dance event—they agreed.

However, he and his colleagues had no prior experience of producing black contemporary dance, but he raised the funds to pay the artists, had a clear idea of what they wanted, and made it happen. Black dance had previously been contained to heritage dance and on a small scale. David and his team wanted to demonstrate that this was limiting and undermining. The collective organising the event had a shared sense of what they wanted and, again, learned by doing. They would seek advice from experts as needed and adopt if the advice was relevant, but they would also do things differently. The shows were a sell out and, the following year, they went on to produce a second successful programme of dance.

David regards the overall learning to be that, sometimes, it is worth stepping into an arena that is outside your field of expertise and comfort; being curious and willing to de-mystify tasks opens up creative opportunities. Generalising from your own experience and knowledge makes you aware of your transferable skills. (Obviously, there are some fields in which there needs to be specialist expertise such as medicine.)

Leadership behaviours that help to implement diversity

It starts with respect for self and others as well as compassion—knowing it is difficult to be free. You need to have a strong self-belief to enable others to realise their own strengths; it allows you to see the potential of others around you even when they doubt themselves. You need to model the behaviours that are needed so that people feel they can have their voices, views, and perspectives can be heard. David learned this by watching and listening to others while being supported by those who believed that we all have agency and the ability to effect change under the right conditions.

If we can stop, see, and value diverse people (including those from working-class backgrounds) in a leadership role, then that is progress. Remembering that you are part of a larger shift for diversity, equity, and inclusion is vital. David was influenced by a statement made by Professor Alvin Poussaint. The Professor stated that it was the duty of every young black person to go out into the world and learn and bring back that knowledge to their village/community. Harnessing collective knowledge and having a shared aspiration are vital for real progress so that it is not tokenistic or short term.

The ability to discriminate is linked to power and the associated rules and parameters. This, for diversity and society, often leads to an imbalance of power as those without it often must comply. It is important to model the positive and be prepared to use your authority to address individuals or groups whose framework or approach is inappropriate and counterproductive. Take time to understand the person/group (realising that their self-interest or fear may ultimately impede them and the organisation's aim), provide opportunities for change but also know that there may come a time when you need to use your authority to confront difficulties.

Don't let the statement 'Rome was not built in a day' prevent you from trying. There are no quick fixes, but we need to keep building on the successes and provide hope.

Addressing negative aspects of leaders and organisations

David's younger self was driven, everything was urgent, and belief in the power of group action was immense. He was not a procrastinator, but he was not as generous as he could have been. However, the early exposure to community activism, academics, and black intellectuals fostered the importance of taking time to reflect, then reassess and realise that there is more than one path to change.

Many leaders believe that they are imposters and that they will be found out. They can also invest vast amounts of energy trying to conceal what they do not know. They often construct and facilitate complex barriers that create a culture of insecurity. Good diversity practice does not thrive in a sea of insecurity and protectionism. It necessitates a belief in individual development and growth, and this empowerment, when shared collectively, creates a groundswell for change. Change that is personal, communal, and structural.

In the process of creating more democratic institutions, leaders need to establish very clear and explicit objectives and outcomes and engage in a shared understanding of what the organisation is trying to achieve. Regardless of where you are leading from, you need to cajole, nudge, persuade, and, on other occasions, sit back and inspire others to take the reins.

Regardless, the message is not to wait for change to evolve casually and in a meandering manner. Work needs to be done within a particular timeframe. All this needs to be handed over to those who will be enacting the objectives and achieving the outcomes, not just be something that the leader knows and believes in. They need to continue their own journey. Although, on occasion (when energies are low), one might need to remind the leadership and the staff of the shared vision and aspirations.

Acting consistently with integrity is vital for leaders. David is a governor of a local school in South London, and he was appointed to ensure that the actions of the school were consistent with its ethos even when expanding.

Currently, David is the Chairperson of Creative Lives, encompassing England, Ireland, Scotland, and Wales. Creative Lives shifted objectives away from a representation role and intermediary for funders to becoming a champion of everyday creativity by ordinary people via greater local democratic engagement. Many people are creating something, often on a pittance, that raises their spirits, hopes, and a personal and collective sense of worth. Other parts of the arts world are now waking up to this important aspect—a good thing if it is not colonised through the act of large institutions determining what is of importance and value.

A framework of shared and inclusive objectives with associated outcomes provides a positive outline with clarity. It helps people understand what the goal is. It also provides you with an arena within which you can address negative behaviours through the regular practice of review and support. Provide ways of learning and time for reflection on how they are working. How are we progressing? What could we do better? This will help people be more accountable, build collective certainty, and enhance inner confidence.

If the negative behaviours persist, it may be necessary to seek human resources advice if it is available. If it isn't, it is necessary to still address the issue and work out what to do with other stakeholders in a less formal setting before acting.

This should be done carefully as it could lead to heightened emotions alongside tough decisions which affect individual lives and futures. You may well have to dismiss someone who has been part of the group and culture, and this is usually more noticeable in smaller organisations. If this happens, then the leadership need to reflect on what happened and learn lessons.

What has hindered diversity, equity and inclusion?

David said, 'Several issues have deterred progress. First, I think there is mass ignorance in this country of the history of its diverse populations as well as a lack of appreciation of the value they bring. Diversity (complex and multi-layered) has often been framed by those in power who have sometimes defined and described it in a limited way for their own purposes. Diversity, or more exactly Diversity, Equity and Inclusion, is about achieving greater social justice and, ultimately, that requires confronting uncomfortable truths.

Diversity and inclusion are important because they go beyond self-interest and profiting just the strong. They take us into the terrain of institutional change and a recognition of the world and the multiple communities and diversities with whom we exist, beyond ourselves. Quick fixes are not sufficient such as appointing a single person, a lone ranger, to change the organisation. The tasks and responsibilities will be too much, and they will inevitably fail. We need to shift to organisation-wide change looking at history, power, purpose, and the toxic cultures that often exist. How do these impact the delivery of the service and who the organisation is serving/working for?

There is no national inclusive vision in the UK that incorporates diversity, and that is not only incredibly myopic, but it also perpetuates conflicts and divides. We need an inclusive vision and purpose with equity as this would generate a different discussion, beyond the gaps of past knowledge into future intent. There is, currently, no proper debate about what good diversity and equity mean for our society. If you have diversity, equity, and inclusion, then it means that you are caring for those whom most systems would ignore or not deem worthy to deserve their current positions.

Some are unable to work through all these complex issues because they come with fixed mindsets or seek simplicity and will leap onto the latest fashionable diversity-related intervention to implement. They should be asking what would work here for these people, with this history, in these circumstances. How do you build collaborations that invest in communities and build local assets, beyond the inevitable short-term intervention? Some want simple tools that will allow them to produce short term change rather than unravel the complex organisational issues that exist and need to be tackled for full diversity.

Lastly, there is fear. Individuals can have no idea how to engage with real change for diversity and they see it as personal, painful conflict as opposed to transformative conflict. It is difficult to discover and unlearn. Changing could be a threat to what they know, on so many levels.'

What more is needed?

David's perspective is, 'Hearts and minds need to be the focus. It is crucial that people are enabled to think critically, learn, and build on mutual benefit. A shared inclusive vision with an honest accounting of the past is required. Embracing the truth should be followed by a focus on building new localised structures for participatory democracy. Empowering unheard voices and lived experiences to participate in reshaping social, economic, and cultural lives is also vital.

Better inclusive governance is needed by encouraging and experimenting with different ways of engagement. Current governance and legislation will inevitably have been heavily influenced by the past and yet are still maintained. Are they fit for purpose? Additionally, it is vital that processes are constructed that create democratic engagement for the many and not just the select few. We also need a shift in structures, otherwise we are at risk of creating singular saviours and reinforcing existing disadvantages.

At Brixton House, the arts centre being built in Brixton, they are exploring different ways in governance, to draw in members of the community to contribute to Brixton House as a cultural hub. They have created working groups that are supported by a lead member of staff and two board members, plus a collection of outsiders with relevant knowledge or experience. By doing this, they will have a different accountability framework—the staff and board members to the community. This ensures that they will remain attentive to what and why they are working, and they will explain and report on the key issues. And this is not the end but just the beginning, more will be done to enfranchise other sections of the community.

A hope for diversity

Fundamentally, we need an inclusive vision for the future that acknowledges the wealth and wrongs of the past. Many diverse people (including those from different races) do not feel that they fully belong in the UK.

At the cultural hub in Brixton, David said 'we can only work towards creating a micro-model of what we hope is possible. We plan to go beyond the physical building and create other spaces in the borough, so that we are programming for the spirit of Brixton and thus bringing in its cultural energy'.

Understanding privilege
Emmicki Roos

'Privilege is when you think something is not a problem, because it's not a problem to you personally.'
—*David Gaider*

What is privilege?

Having worked in gender equality and organisational development for almost 15 years, I have come across many challenges related to leadership and unhealthy work environments. A key universal challenge across organisations is a failure to understand privilege, the power structures associated with that privilege, and its effects on the individual and the organisation.

Whenever I bring up the concept of privilege in a workshop, there are usually some objections from one or two of the participants. For example, when a participant said: '"I'm a white middle-aged man, but my life has been very difficult. I had a tough childhood, I was unemployed for a long time, I'm divorced, and recently had cancer, so I'm definitely not privileged.' I answered him the same way I always do when this comes up. 'Privilege does not mean that your life has been easy, that you have not struggled. It simply means that your sex and the colour of your skin has not made it harder.' This notion that having privilege somehow means that we have lived a carefree life without any struggles seems to be common and is one of the many ways in which we distance ourselves from it.

Perhaps we fear that acknowledging our privilege to others makes us vulnerable to critique and responsible for creating a more level playing field. To some extent this is correct; while being privileged gives us a head start in life, it comes with a responsibility. Let's have a deeper look into what it is, and then we can look at how to understand our own privilege, and strengthen our golden sides and leadership skills.

Privilege is often invisible to those who have it and the more we have, the harder it generally becomes to recognise our own advantages. It can be divided into two sets: that we are born with and that we have some degree of influence over. Most privilege is not earned or something we have control over and is related to characteristics like our race, sex, sexual orientation, and the social class into which we were born. Privilege that we may have some degree of influence over includes our level of education, income, and looks. While recognising that some people can influence their degree of privilege, it is important to understand that, for most people, this is not possible. The society, community, clan, social class, and family we were born into does, to a large extent, influence our life chances. A good example of this is level of education. A survey by Statistics Sweden found that 80 percent of adults with two highly educated parents have a university or college degree, as compared to 25 percent of the adults if neither parent was highly educated.

To simplify it, privilege is power and is often a form of injustice that separates people into those who have it and those who don't have it. What makes it complex is the fact that one person can both be privileged and unprivileged at the same time. A black man can be underprivileged in a predominantly white society, for instance in the United States, due to racism, and yet be privileged in the black community of that society because of sexism and the fact that he was born a man. While the racism black men can face in the United States is unique and accounts for them being both black and a man, it is in some ways different than the racism towards black women. To understand privilege, we therefore need to have an intersectional approach summarised well by Dr Greta Bauer, in a publication by the Institute of Gender and Health, Canadian Institute of Health Research.

The term, intersectionality, was first coined in 1989 by Columbia Law School professor Kimberlé W. Crenshaw to describe the realities of African American women who experience intersecting, concurrent, and cumulative forms of discrimination and subjugation; racism for being black and sexism for being women. Intersectionality describes how race, class, sex, and other characteristics or identities intersect with one another and overlap. It allows us to see that an individual's experiences are not just the total of their different identities or characteristics but constitute intersections of axes of social power. For example, lesbian women's experiences of the workplace may be different from those of homosexual men and non-lesbian women. Similarly, Asian lesbian women's experiences may be different to white lesbian women's experiences and so on. The wheel of privilege/power, originally developed by educator Sylvia Duckworth and later adapted by the Canadian Institute of Health Research in 2021 to describe the axes of social power in Canada, illustrates this and helps us understand what is intersectionality.

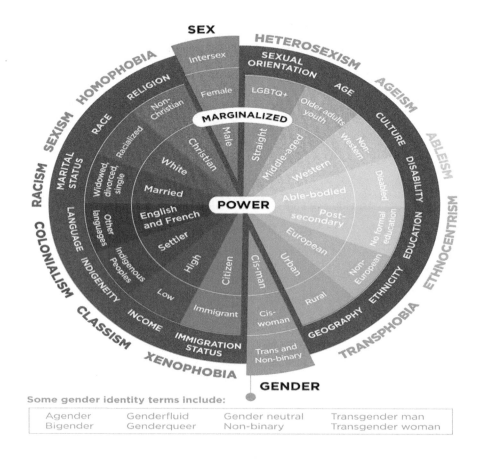

(Cisgender (or 'cis') is a term used to describe people whose gender identity aligns with the sex they were assigned at birth, while transgender (or 'trans') is used to describe people whose gender identity and sex assigned at birth do not align.)

As we continue to explore the consequences of privilege and our own role, it is good to revisit the wheel of privilege/power to remind ourselves of the need for an intersectional approach.

Why does it matter?

'When you're accustomed to privilege, equality feels like oppression.'
—*Chris Boeskool*

Now that we have explored what privilege is, let's turn to why it matters for us as individuals, members of organisations, and leaders. The golden sides described in Chapter Two—compassion, inclusivity, and diversity—are necessary traits and values for any individual to function well in a group with others. Compassion relates to respect and treating others fairly and with kindness, while inclusion and diversity relate to equality and power sharing. If we are unaware of our privileges, others' lack of privilege, and the hierarchies of power in our organisation, we are bound to reinforce those dynamics, whether we intend to or not.

Ultimately, these power structures lead to discrimination, inequality, and an unhealthy work environment. Hence the work we do as leaders, to examine our own privilege and the power structures in our organisation, is so important to promote compassion, inclusion, and diversity. Examining our own privilege may be uncomfortable at first, but it is necessary, and there are no shortcuts if we want to lead by example and internalise the true meaning of these golden sides of leadership.

Why can examining one's privilege be uncomfortable or unsettling? Perhaps because when we allow ourselves to see our privileges clearly, we realise that some of the power and benefits we have is at the expense of those who are less privileged and, as a result, have less power and benefits. Social power is like apple pie. There is only one pie and only so many pieces to be divided. If you have more pieces than your fair share, someone else will automatically have less.

The only way those with less power can have more, is if those with more power give up some of theirs. It is simple mathematics, and yet it is often met with resistance. Chris Boeskool, a contributor at HuffPost explained it well when he wrote: 'Equality can feel like oppression. But it's not. What you're feeling is just the discomfort of losing a little bit of your privilege.'

Any process that requires us to change our worldview and our behaviour is by default uncomfortable. Especially if that process leads to us giving up some of our privilege. So, what are the incentives for examining one's privilege and having the awareness that it brings us as leaders? It will allow us to see the world and our organisation with new eyes; and behaviours that have previously been a mystery to us will be easier to interpret. We will, hopefully, become more compassionate people and our leadership will have a greater impact on the people in our organisation. Ultimately, it will give us the insight to replace outdated norms, which benefit the few, with norms that promote inclusivity, diversity, and compassion and benefit the many and our organisation.

As well as making the workplace more enjoyable and a place where our staff are motivated and thrive, there are financial incentives for leading a diverse and inclusive organisation. A Boston Consulting Group study found that companies with diverse management teams are more innovative and as a result have 19 percent higher revenues. More broadly, it is estimated that closing the gender gap in the private sector globally would add $28 trillion to the value of the economy by 2025. This 26 percent increase in value re-inforces what research from multiple disciplines has already established: that gender equality and diversity is a recipe for growth and prosperity.

This is also true when we look at peace and security. A publication by the World Bank shows that there is a strong link between the level of gender inequality and the likelihood that a country will be involved in conflict and use military force as a first response. While women's equal participation in peace processes is a right and, as such, a goal (in itself), there is also research showing that women's equal participation has a positive impact on the longevity of peace agreements. When women are left out, peace agreements are less likely to be reached and implemented. While countries and organisations differ, there are many synergies and lessons to be learned about human behaviour and what creates the best foundation for a healthy organisation. There is no way to get around the fact that privileges and existing power dynamics lead to inequality and discrimination and that we must be aware of this to build healthy and prosperous organisations and societies.

How do we understand our own privilege?

> 'Being privileged doesn't mean that you are always wrong and people without privilege are always right. It means that there is a good chance you are missing a few very important pieces of the puzzle.'
> —Ijeoma Oluo, author of So You Want to Talk About Race

Having explored what privilege is and why it matters, we will now delve into how we can become aware of our own privilege and the power structures around us. Understanding one's privilege is at the core of the French film *Je ne suis pas un homme facile*, (*I Am Not an Easy Man*) from 2018. In the film, we get to know Damien, who is a shameless chauvinist and has all the benefits of living in a gender unequal society. Damien frequently objectifies and discriminates against women and views children and taking care of the home as a woman's domain. One day, Damien bumps into a streetlight and passes out. When he wakes up, it is in a parallel universe, where stereotypical gender roles are reversed, and women have the power.

Suddenly, Damien is the one to experience sexism, discrimination, and sexual harassment; this opens his eyes to the privilege he used to have, the rights he used to take for granted, and how gender inequality affects women. While Damien had to accidently bump his head into a streetlight to see his own privilege and the power structures around him, we can explore our own privilege in less painful ways.

While some simple tools can help us to get started, we must accept that this is a long-term learning process. This process requires us to test our assumptions about the self and others and use observation to gather useful information about the power structures that surround us. Sometimes this learning about our privilege is planned and sometimes it happens organically.

Dr Peggy McIntosh, senior researcher, and former Associate Director of the Wellesley Center for Women started examining and working on her own privilege as a white American decades ago. In 1989, she wrote:

'I have come to see white privilege as an invisible package of unearned assets which I can count on cashing in each day, but about which I was 'meant' to remain oblivious. White privilege is like an invisible weightless knapsack of special provisions, maps, passports, codebooks, visas, clothes, tools and blank checks. I decided to try to work on myself at least by identifying some of the daily effects of white privilege in my life.'

To make her own skin-colour privilege visible, while at the same time having an intersectional approach, McIntosh started to list some of the conditions in life which she takes for granted as a white person. In her own analysis, the conditions that she lists are conditions her African American colleagues, friends, and acquaintances may not count on because of racism. Here are a few examples of the conditions she identified as being associated with her white privilege:

'If a traffic cop pulls me over or if the IRS audits my tax return, I can be sure I haven't been singled out because of my race.

Whether I use checks, credit cards, or cash, I can count on my skin color not to work against the appearance of financial reliability.

I am never asked to speak for all the people of my racial group.'

Exercise: Knapsack

Like Peggy McIntosh, think about some of the circumstances in your life that you count on or take for granted. Then reflect on whether you would be able to count on these conditions if your race and/or sex was different. Now write down some of the ones you think you would not be able to count on if your race and/or sex was different than it is. Remember to have an intersectional approach!

What can we learn from Peggy McIntosh's work in 1989? Aside from how to reflect on our own privilege, her work illustrates the importance of examining one's privilege even if you have one or more characteristics and identities associated with less privilege and social power. McIntosh is a woman and had, herself, experienced discrimination based on her sex. Compared to most white men she had less privilege and social power, yet in comparison to her African American colleagues and friends, she had white privilege and often more social power. While we may be subjected to discrimination and lack privilege in some ways, it does not give us a free pass to disregard the privilege we do have and the responsibilities that come with it.

Even if we have not been subjected to discrimination based on our sex or race, most of us have experienced situations where we have less social power than we are used to. A former colleague experienced this when he went from working in civil society to working as a civilian expert for the armed forces. As a white heterosexual man with an academic education, he was used to peers greeting him and being listened to at work. In the new work environment, where a military background was the norm, he felt that he constantly had to prove himself and justify his existence in the organisation. Military colleagues would ignore him in every day social situations and refuse to greet him in the lunch queue. He felt that the social relationships and codes formed over decades of service in the armed forces were much more important than competence and whatever expertise he could bring to the organisation. This made him nervous about meeting new groups in the organisation and made him change his body language and verbal utterances to try to raise his social status. Years later he summarised his emotions as feeling belittled and marginalised. Maybe you have experienced something similar; first month in a new school; in the soccer team; meeting your in-laws for the first time—or at a social gathering where you don't know anyone?

Exercise: Shark tank

Think about a situation like the one described in the example above where you had less social power than you are used to. Write down a couple of words/lines describing how that situation made you feel and how it affected your sense of Self.

Having reflected on how this situation made you feel and how it affected your sense of Self, now imagine that this experience would not be a one-off where you could go back to the social power you were used to. Imagine that the lower social power would be permanent and that nothing you could do would alter the fact that characteristics associated with you like your sexual orientation, sex, and race would lead to various forms of marginalisation and discrimination throughout your lifetime. Imagine how this would affect your sense of Self, confidence, relationships, outlook on life, and psyche.

While this exercise cannot replace or simulate real lived racism, sexism, or other forms of discrimination, it is a simple way for us to use our own experiences in life to strengthen our compassion and understanding of privilege. We are constantly subjected to experiences and situations where we can choose to examine our own privilege and assumptions, and let the lessons learned guide our leadership. Let me give you an example.

A couple of years ago, I worked with a manager at a senior level who was informed that several women in his organisation had been subjected to sexual harassment, blackmail, discrimination, and abuse of power by the same perpetrator, who was one of their colleagues. The women had been threatened by the perpetrator and his allies in the organisation, and one of the female staff was suicidal because of this. The women wanted the abuse to stop but were too scared of retaliation to submit formal complaints. There was also a lack of trust that senior management would handle their complaints correctly and that they would act.

When I informed the manager of the women's situation and fears (with their permission), I expected him to react with compassion and understanding. Instead, he was completely oblivious to their experience and could not understand their fear of reporting. He was unable to see his own privilege, as a white, senior, middle-aged man from an advantaged background, in relation to these women who were junior staff belonging to a traditional and clan-based community where the family's honour depends on women's perceived behaviour.

The manager finally agreed to talk to the perpetrator and as some of his violent behaviour had been caught on video, he promised that this man would not have his contract renewed at the end of the year. After having left the organisation, I made a visit the year after and was surprised to see that the perpetrator was still working there. I confronted the manager who said that he had been 'rehabilitated' and could stay on. I asked if that meant that he had received counselling, and he had not. The women were still living in fear, and nothing had changed for them. The actions of the manager and his peers had just confirmed their fears and made them feel even more hopeless and marginalised.

This example can teach us something about privilege and the assumptions we all make about other people's experience. We tend to base our understanding of the world and our organisations on our own experiences which are often unique and cannot be generalised to others. An example of this is how often people are perceived differently by those at different levels of the organisational hierarchy. While senior staff may perceive someone as polite, friendly, and charming, it is not uncommon that the same person is perceived as arrogant and a bully by more junior staff.

Is this because the person's behaviour is interpreted differently at separate levels? More likely than not, the answer rather lies in the fact that most people alter their behaviour depending on who they are interacting with and are more respectful when engaging with people who are their peers and are perceived to have more social power, as opposed to people who are perceived to have less social power. Most of us are not bullies, but we all do this to some degree as we have been socialised to cling to those with a large degree of social power.

When I want to know someone's true character in an organisation, I don't ask senior management or the person's peers; I talk to the interns, cleaners, and assistants. When our experience is based on privilege, which translates into a large degree of social power, we tend to become blind to the fact that others in our organisations experience people, interactions, and situations differently.

What could the manager, in our example about sexual harassment, have done differently? Instead of assuming that these women experienced the workplace the same way he did and had the same agency he did to report abuse, the manager could have examined his own privilege and reflected on the power structures in the organisation and how they affected these women. Hopefully, such reflections would have yielded a more compassionate response and actions to ensure that the rights of the women were protected and that the perpetrator was held accountable. Instead, his non-action enabled the perpetrator and reinforced discriminatory power structures.

Additionally, his failure to act was deeply unethical, unprofessional, and a violation of the organisation's policies. In another country, with more progressive legislation, it could have also constituted a crime as he and the organisation had failed to take action to prevent and respond to violence in the workplace.

There are many ways of exploring one's privilege and the power structures that surround us. Now we will explore a method that we will call 'doing detective work'. This method is based on observation and has been adapted from the work of Dr Eva Amundsdotter, a Swedish researcher focused on leadership and organisational development with long experience of training leaders in gender-responsive leadership.

Exercise: Doing detective work

For the next couple of weeks, pay extra attention to how your colleagues interact in daily work activities, such as physical and online meetings and tasks. What privileges or biases might be influencing team dynamics and individual behaviour? Are men and women treated differently? Are junior staff treated differently to senior staff? Are white colleagues treated differently to other colleagues? Also reflect about yourself and note down if you are treating colleagues differently based on these characteristics and associated levels of social power and, if so, why you are doing this? You can also pay attention to other characteristics like sexual orientation, age, and disability. Remember to have an intersectional approach!

Pay attention to:

- Division of tasks and responsibilities—who does what?
- Who volunteers or is assigned to prepare agendas, take notes, write reports, make coffee?
- Who talks in meetings?
- Whose ideas and suggestions are being picked up?
- Who interrupts whom and who is quiet?
- Who takes decisions?

What did you observe? Please write down a few sentences.

If you feel comfortable doing this with a peer or friend, you can each do this in your organisations/teams and then meet up for a coffee to discuss your observations and reflections.

How can we use our understanding of privilege for good?

Now that we have a basic understanding of what privilege is, why it matters, and our own privilege and the power dynamics in our own organisation, we will turn to how we can use this understanding for good. We will also explore how this can help us reinforce and maintain our golden sides and enable us to lead with compassion.

Let's begin with an example of how a leader used his privilege for good. In the publication *Better Peace Tool* by the International Civil Society Action Network (ICAN), Anawarul Chowdhury, Former Under-Secretary-General of the United Nations recalled how President Nelson Mandela used his influence while mediating peace negotiations. 'Mandela briefed us in the Security Council and said the men weren't willing to involve women. In the evening, he would sit and listen to [the women] and in the morning he suggested [their points] as if they were his ideas, and the men loved them. Eventually, he told [the men] these were the women's points, not his . . . that is how he brought women in to the final two rounds.'

Speaking on behalf of others who are excluded from meetings and processes can be problematic. However, if it is used to ensure that they can join the meeting and speak for themselves, it can be a fruitful strategy. While we may not be as powerful as President Nelson Mandela, most of us have enough power to make a positive mark on our organisations and communities.

The easiest way to do this, which will have an immediate impact on your colleagues and your organisation, is to reinforce what is said by colleagues with less social power and give them due credit. For example, if a colleague is interrupted and not listened to, you can say: 'I think X had something important to say, I suggest we all pay attention,' or 'X raised a very important point...' or 'As X said...'

A common situation which many women have experienced is having their ideas stolen by a male colleague. During a workshop on how to promote gender equality in the workplace I facilitated an exercise on this called 'Gender Glasses'. A group was given a script and asked to play out a scene for the rest of the participants illustrating this. In the script, managers are discussing a problem when the only woman suggests a solution. The male managers ignore her and talk over her, trying to silence her. Then a male manager copies the solution presented by the female manager and offers it as his own idea. He is praised and applauded by the male managers who think that his solution is brilliant. After the script had been played out for the audience, they were able to share their observations of what had just happened and how one could have intervened if in the room.

Everyone agreed that reinforcing her idea in the first place could have prevented the situation from escalating. When the male manager had stolen her idea and was praised when presenting it as his own, one could have also intervened and said: 'This is a great idea, but how does it differ from what X just said?' or 'Thank you X for making the initial suggestion which allowed us to continue brainstorming around a solution.'

Another way that we can support our colleagues with less social power is by ensuring that they have access to growth opportunities at work. They might benefit from having a mentor, and perhaps this is a role you can take. By sharing our knowledge and networks we can open doors for them that otherwise would be closed. Kamala Harris's mother told her, when she became Vice President of the United States in 2021, 'Kamala, you may be the first to do many things, but make sure you are not the last.'

Another situation where we can apply our knowledge about privilege is when we are invited to speak on a panel or at a conference which lacks diversity. This happened to me a couple of years ago when I was invited to sit on a panel to discuss the security situation for women in Afghanistan. While flattered, I politely refused the offer because there were no Afghans, or Afghan women on the panel. Instead, I sent the organisers a list of names of representatives from Afghan women's organisations and suggested that they contact them.

We can also use our knowledge to be careful with our assumptions and, instead of assuming that others are experiencing the organisation or a situation the same way we do, we can invite them to share their experiences and needs. Ensure that there is a safe space and that they are listened to without judgment. If they prefer to be anonymous and are uncomfortable with sharing their perspectives in front of others, an option is to create a mailbox where they can share their views anonymously.

While these examples are easy ways to use our knowledge of privilege for good, we must keep in mind that privilege is about power and that we will not change unequal power structures that lead to discrimination and oppression without challenging our own and others' privilege. To do this we must be willing to give up our own privilege, even if it hurts. We also need to have uncomfortable conversations with our peers, colleagues, friends, partners, and children about privilege and the inequality to which it leads. This might be intimidating at first but can be a great way to make our relationships and conversations more profound and meaningful and will likely lead to new insights and perspectives.

Now that we have explored some simple ways that we can use our understanding of privilege for good, it is time to wrap up so you can start testing your understanding of privilege in real life. When we continually challenge ourselves to examine our own privilege and the power structures around us, the way we perceive ourselves and the world around us changes. We will see things that we have never noticed before. While this can be perceived by some of us as a burden, it is not.

It is a form of superpower which enables us to be the best versions of ourselves and do better in our organisations. Remember this as you move forward and be confident in your ability to apply what you have learned.

Human resources perspectives for healthy leadership
Michael Emery

Human resources departments have a vital function in any organisation. They are the intersection for many staff and an integral part of the operationalisation of the purpose and functions of the organisation.

Inevitably, they outline what is expected in terms of appropriate actions, behaviours, and consequences if the codes of conduct are not followed. In terms of the use and implementation for healthy leadership and organisations, it is often Human Resources that is key and vital.

Michael Emery is an expert and senior Human Resources Director who is currently with IOM (UN Migration). He has a wealth of experience in various parts of the UN. Here is a summary of Michael's perspectives on key issues, which will provide us with some useful insights to enhancing and developing healthy leadership and organisations.

Leadership journey

We asked Michael to first help us understand his background and key leadership qualities. In 1989, he was working as a teacher, had had a tough day, and this coincided with a discussion with his school principal about his teaching plans for the next year. He said that he would like to volunteer in mission schools, perhaps in North-West Australia, in schools for Aboriginal pupils. To his surprise, the following week, he was offered a post in central Liberia. He thought, 'Why not?' and accepted even though he had to look up the country in an atlas. He sold up, was on a flight to Liberia and read in *The Guardian* that about 5,000 people had been killed in the civil war in the country's north.

On arrival in Liberia, he was reassured by those who met him that it was simply a border skirmish and nothing to worry about. Six weeks later, he was out of a job. His students had either been conscripted to be child soldiers or were refugees in neighbouring Guinea. He could return to Australia and look for temporary work or stay in Liberia and find work there.

On the advice of a friend, Michael went to the UN compound in Liberia and was asked to help with food distribution at the national stadium the following day. Initially, he thought this would be a simple task, but it turned to be much larger—for 10,000 people. He was then hired to work in emergency coordination and remained in Liberia, then evacuated and worked in Guinea and then returned to Liberia for almost three years.

Michael was still interested in indigenous education and went back to Australia to work as the head of Aboriginal Education for the South Australia Catholic Education Office. A year later, Michael was contacted by the UN and asked to go to Yugoslavia to work in training. He accepted and spent two years there and later moved to New York to improve pre-deployment training for civilian police, who were often part of peace-keeping missions such as the one deployed to Bosnia after the Dayton Peace Accords.

This period galvanised in Michael that he wanted to work in human resources and so he studied, part time, for a Master's in Organisational Development and Training while returning to the classroom to teach. He then worked as an emergency coordinator for CARE Australia in ex-Yugoslavia and East Timor.

From this post, he became Head of Training for the UN Peacekeeping mission in East Timor. Sérgio Vieira de Mello, Special Representative of the Secretary General (SRSG) and Head of the UN Mission, advised him to move on from training to human resources, as there would be greater career possibilities. Michael followed this advice and subsequently worked in New York as Head of Career Development for UN Peacekeeping and then to the United Nations Development Programmes (UNDP) as Head of Recruitment, which was an interesting five years.

All of Michael's subsequent posts were and are at the Director of Human Resources level for IOM, then the UN Population Fund (UNFPA) and returning to IOM, where he currently works. His in-depth field experience helped him understand the nuances of such operations as well knowing and understanding the emergency and inter-agency context. These have proved invaluable for his responsibilities as a global Director of Human Resources.

Key leadership qualities

Over the years, Michael's qualities have developed and been refined through experience. The first quality he now has, is to practise humility with empathy but not cower. With this, you seek to first understand and unpack other's perspectives, especially when deciding. This includes being a good listener and being able to discern the underlying feelings and thoughts that are being conveyed, not just what is said verbally.

Second, maintaining a sense of humour and not taking yourself too seriously is vital. Otherwise, you are at risk of having an over-inflated ego.

It is also crucial to have a clear vision, including for your function, that you articulate to your team, and this must be inextricably linked to the ability to innovate. If you are within a system, there is a responsibility to improve and make a difference to that system. You need to be able to say, when you leave, that you left the system in better shape. That is the challenge.

Motivation and inspiration

Seeing injustice has remained a significant motivator for Michael. There were days, during his work, where he saw clear injustice and these memories remain as motivation.

He saw abject poverty and instances of injustice during his time in Liberia, including the use of child soldiers. 'To take someone's childhood away is evil, and this childhood can never be regained.' Another injustice was the role that multi-national companies had in contributing to the war, by being complicit in the illicit sale of 'blood timber' for weapons. 'The instant losers were the environment and the people of Liberia.' Another memory is visiting a location in Algeria where people from Western Sahara had been refugees for 25 years because of a complex political situation and there was 'no end in sight' and people were being sustained by the humanitarian multilateral system.

These experiences also contributed to his commitment to the efforts and effectiveness of multilateralism. He was part of UN operations that made tangible differences in Ex-Yugoslavia, Liberia, and East Timor (which was successfully closed at the end of its mandate).

Individuals have also been sources of motivation and inspiration. Even though he did not work with them substantially, he was inspired by working with Ex-Secretary General Kofi Annan and Sérgio Vieira de Mello whose last post was as Head of the UN Mission in Iraq.

Michael was and is encouraged greatly by national staff with whom he has worked, knowing that he came to work to make things better for them. There was also fun in their collaboration.

In his life, there have been strong women who have shaped him—his Irish and Lebanese grandmothers and his mother who was a remarkable, progressive educationalist and feminist. There are others who have been and are real role models, mentors, and with whom he could touch base and discuss ideas—Ross Mountain, Bill Swing, and Douglas Manson being some of the few.

We thank Michael for sharing his history and this helps us learn about the importance of lessons, experience, and having people and events be and remain as motivators. In the following sections, Michael shares his views on aspects of healthy leadership and healthy organisations.

Obtaining healthy leadership and organisations

As well as the qualities noted above, there is first the need to have a culture of recognition. People appreciate being recognised, and this was something his mother would do in her classrooms. In every lesson, she would say something positive about each child.

True and inclusive empowerment is needed. When he worked in Aboriginal education, as part of a Royal Commission into Aboriginal Deaths in Custody, he helped to set up mechanisms, where there had been none, for parents to understand and take part in decision making in schools. At Sérgio Vieira de Mello's memorial service in East Timor, the words spoken by his cleaning lady are still remembered for their message more than those from others of greater seniority. Empowerment must be holistic and implemented such that people feel they can have their voice heard and not be frightened.

Celebrating and not judging cultural differences is important, including in the multilateral UN system. In healthy organisations, diversity needs to be cherished and encouraged so that there is much better engagement.

COVID has highlighted the necessity to be agile in thinking at all levels so that you can adjust and move as the winds change. Otherwise, there is a risk of failure such as Kodak who did not recognise the importance of digitalisation.

While we need to pay attention to advances in technology and innovation, e.g. AI, healthy organisations that thrive are the ones that keep the human in human resources. 'We are dealing with people, not just market efficiencies and bottom lines.'

Promoting the use of positive golden behaviours

This can be achieved by recognition and highlighting champions and clearing out negative shadow behaviours professionally. At a presentation, a head of HR in a company that sold drill bits shifted the culture through changing the reward system. Previously, only salespeople received bonuses and there was no sharing. A new bonus system was introduced that had three elements: teamwork, career opportunities for staff, and sales, each with a maximum score of three, and these were then multiplied to get a final score. Thus, if you got zero for teamwork, the overall total would be zero. Some embraced this and others left to be replaced by those willing to take part in the new culture.

At IOM, the incoming performance management tool will have multi-rater feedback to obtain an empowerment and engagement index. Responders will have to answer questions about their manager such as whether they have team meetings, take responsibility when there is an issue, and recognise and acknowledge work. This will, hopefully, lead to a positive sense of competition and the use of positive behaviour through encouragement and nudging.

It is important to model the behaviours you want. Your actions as a leader will contribute to the perception that staff will have of you and, thus, your leadership. Downsizing while having your office expensively refurbished will inevitably lead to negative perceptions of the leader.

It is also key to address the fact that some will be unwilling to let go of their use of negative and toxic actions. This should be done in a professional and considerate manner while being clear that such behaviours are not acceptable.

To discourage negative behaviours

It is imperative to act and have a mechanism through which people can highlight the negative shadow behaviours. Equally, there must be awareness raising of what behaviours are expected through staff training and development including considering possible cultural differences in what is acceptable behaviour. People from two different cultures could disagree on whether shouting at staff is acceptable. Staff development and training needs to be adequately resourced so that people can understand what is expected. In his first term as HR Director, IOM, Michael highlighted that there should not be negative or sarcastic signs in people's offices, and this was followed.

Addressing the persistent use of negative shadow behaviours

Each situation is different and so it is vital to unpack and understand why the behaviours are or are seen to be negative. For example, poor performance may be just that and not abuse of authority as claimed. But it is important to explore thoroughly.

If the behaviour is genuinely negative, then discussions should be held with the person to raise awareness of the negativity of the behaviours and their impact on people in that person's immediate circle. The person should then be given the possibility of redemption and the chance to make a change as they may not have realised or recognised that it was prohibited or negative. Opportunities for improvement must be given but parameters for action also need to be set if there is no change. People need to understand the potential consequences if they do not change.

This approach needs to be utilised at all levels of management so that people are helped to address their negative behaviours rather than simply trying to move the person elsewhere. Doing so will lead to a healthy organisation where all understand what is expected of them and that negative shadow behaviours will be addressed.

There needs to be an internal justice system (ombudspersons, a place for people to report and have their concerns heard, investigation unit, etc.) Some of the existing ones need to improve so that there are better and faster outcomes of concerns raised.

Hope for healthy leadership and organisations

We need a healthy leadership and organisation index that provides a framework within which leaders and organisations can create their own standards and expectations. This will create aspirations to live up to. One of these is the hope that the voice of people in organisations is genuinely included and another is that their voices will be heard as part of the day-to-day practice of the organisation and its leaders.

Agent of Change: Richard Beckhard

Dick Beckhard was very much a pioneer, whose work and ideas informed and steered many people. Unfortunately, his name and work are not easily recalled these days, but those who work in organisational change and development have greatly benefitted from the stage that his ideas built for us.

His autobiography is aptly titled, *Agent of Change: My Life, My Practice.* This summary is an attempt to honour Dick Beckhard and his contribution, as well as being a reminder to all of us to know about and respect our past.

His aim was to 'influence organisations to function in a more humane as well as high performing mode'. Dick Beckhard was a powerful advocate of learning by doing and that life (work and personal) comprised social systems of relationships to be managed and which required commitment. His background included privilege and its loss, because of the stock market crash in 1929. He was a natural entrepreneur in various settings, including theatre, the Red Cross, training and then working with organisations.

He taught at the Sloan Management School, Massachusetts Institute of Technology (MIT), and used many innovative approaches to get the best from his students. This included the use of the *pensée*, a paper that students were asked to write about the meaning of the course for them instead of a more straightforward assessment. Dick Beckhard retired, as Professor, from the Sloan School in 1984 and he was honoured with an MIT-wide celebratory day where there were presentations and gatherings around his accomplishments. His humility about his impact came through clearly in his autobiography when he said that to be honoured thus was beyond his 'fondest dream'. The School still awards the Richard Beckhard Memorial Prize for the most outstanding article in the MIT Sloan Management Review for that year.

He helped to shape the Office for Public Management (OPM) and the Public Management Foundation in England, which were founded by Greg Parston and Laurie McMahon. The spirit and culture of OPM were based on helping organisations to 'manage for social result' while aiming for financial probity. At its zenith, OPM personnel were influential in many of the innovations in public services in England and other countries. The culture of OPM enabled staff (Fellows, Senior Fellows, and Directors) to feel free and explore while working and securing projects with the public sector. There were regular monthly days at which the group was encouraged to continue the zeitgeist and learn. Eventually, OPM became an employee-owned organisation.

Dick Beckhard used and created many approaches that still have validity today. These include utilising the Blake Mouton Managerial Grid that is focussed around two factors: concern for people and for production. He was also a proponent of the force field analysis method developed by Kurt Lewin. Dick Beckhard's own change formula, Dissatisfaction x Vision x First Steps > Resistance to Change, is still revered in the field.

Dick Beckhard envisaged organisations as a complex of systems: social (identity and purpose with a need for coordination), political, and input-output. He devised and used a change management model which influenced those that were later produced: considering the present and the future, as well as the transition in between. He recommended an assessment of the commitment and responsibility of key actors in a change process.

His aspiration for effective organisations was that they would be purposeful and goal oriented, that work be allocated and resourced as needed and not by power, and that decisions be made on sources of information and not on hierarchy. Sensible reward systems—both intrinsic and extrinsic—would exist alongside open communication; conflict was managed not suppressed or avoided. Management would attempt to support everyone's identity, integrity, and freedom. Work and rewards were organised to maintain these values and that the organisation operated in a learning mode.

Richard Beckhard Memorial Service—Trinity Church, Manhattan, 13 February 2000

My name is Greg Parston. I'm from London, England, where—over the past 12 years—Dick Beckhard worked with me and others to help create the Office for Public Management and the Public Management Foundation, of which Dick was a founding trustee. Others have spoken of Dick's passion for networking, but I would like to talk about Dick's passion for islands—this island, Manhattan, but also the island of Britain. For before working with me, Dick worked for many years establishing himself as one of the most influential change agents in British industry.

Dick worked with the British National Health Service, the UK Cabinet Office and the Metropolitan Police. He also supported Royal Dutch Shell, where he met Wendy Pritchard, who was to become a dear friend and co-author. But most notably, Dick worked for over 30 years to help shape and reshape ICI, and during that time was special advisor to six chairmen, including Sir John Harvey Jones, Britain's best-known manager.

Sir John, on learning of Dick's death a few weeks ago, wrote to me to say, 'I am sure I do not have to tell you what an unbelievable man we have lost—Dick did so much good for so many people.'

Some of Dick's American friends may not know a lot about his passion for the isles of Britain; others may not know about his passion for the islands of the sea—for Tortolla, Anegada and Jost van Dyke of the Virgin Islands. For as well as using sailing as a metaphor in much of his development work, Dick was a sailor for real. As a man who spent much of his life behind the throne—working as a facilitator and coach to help others who were trying to control their organisations, when he was behind the wheel of a fifty-foot Bennateau at full sail, it was Dick who was in control. And for those of you who (like me) had the pleasure of sharing a week sailing with Skipper Dick, I am sure you will agree that it was an unforgettable and a once-in-a-lifetime experience.

But what marks Dick especially for me are two things. First was his energetic feistiness—always willing to have another go, run another seminar, have another brainstorming session and always ready to change the best-laid plans and formats if he thought the learning could be more dramatic, more effective, more enduring. But he did not seek out attention, as many of his guru contemporaries do. One of his lasting lessons to me is, 'Don't compete with your clients for fame.' He always put them centre stage.

But second and more important was Dick's value-driven view of management and of organisations and of their roles in improving society. He often said to me he hoped his life would be remembered for having helped 'too-bureaucratic' and 'too-distant' organisations become more human and more humane. He always challenged his clients at that level.

But whether we were clients or colleagues, students or fellow sailors, Dick was our trusted counsel, the one who put our concerns at the centre of the map, helped us learn more about ourselves, and was always willing to share his knowledge and his experience to help us make our lives more value-driven too.

Like you, I will miss Dick, but we will never lose him.

Changing habits (cognitively and practically)
Jamie Ripman

Over the past 25 years, I've been working as a coach, facilitator, and leadership development consultant and have been particularly interested in the practice of leadership. What does leadership look like, sound like, and feel like as we execute our own leadership and experience the leadership of others?

Before I moved into this field, I trained in the performing arts at the Bristol Old Vic Theatre School (England) and worked professionally as an actor, writer, and director. And my work in leadership development has always been informed by this experience. In my occupation as an actor there were some fascinating elements to the process of becoming a different character (the essence of acting) when, in the rehearsal room, you began to make the shift from 'performing' the character to 'becoming' the character. The performed version was consciously created as you experimented with different 'intentions' and mindsets, as well as exploring different physical and vocal energies and habits. Then, after a period of time, the new ways of thinking, speaking, and behaving emerged more unconsciously after several days and weeks of practice.

Alongside these experiences, I've also always been a keen enthusiast of playing, watching, and studying sport, where there are many similarities in the way that sports players develop their expertise. In this field, the term 'muscle memory' is often used to describe the unconscious behaviour that enables elite players to dazzle us with their amazing skills. There are also many other disciplines from which we understand that new, authentic, and sustainable behaviours can be developed through practice, rehearsal, and experimentation.

And as we have reported elsewhere in this book, these experiences are all now supported by the neuroscience that has assisted us to recognise that our minds, emotions, and bodies are helpfully flexible and plastic as we endeavour to enact new thoughts and behaviours. How can we transfer these processes into the field of leadership development that will enable us successfully to change our habits for the better?

So, from my days as a drama school student, I've always been interested in the connections between mind, body, and voice. In our development of new characters, we were encouraged to explore the mental, physical, and vocal shifts needed to become other people. To become another person, we needed to work out how that person thought, looked, and sounded. This model has stuck with me, as I now work with leaders to help them become other or better versions of themselves.

What's helpful about this very simple model is that the three areas interconnect and, by changing one area, there will often be an effect on another. Take, for example, a leader who wants to build more empathy and compassion into their daily interactions. This new habit could begin with a shift of mindset, where the leader might focus initially on the extent to which they are considering the perspectives of others before acting. Developing more awareness and understanding of how others are thinking and feeling about anything is a cognitive exercise that is likely to lead to a behavioural change where the leader asks more questions, gives more eye contact, speaks less, pauses more, and softens their vocal tones in their interactions with others.

Similarly, a journey towards exhibiting more empathy and compassion could start with a behavioural practice of simply pausing and asking, 'What do you think?' before waiting for a response. When others feel that someone is showing an interest in them and is prepared to listen, they will often behave differently towards the leader who, over time, is rewarded for the shift in the behaviour which can then lead to a mindset shift about the value of understanding the perspectives of others. This then reinforces the behaviour which gets used and practised and, over time, becomes an embedded and authentic part of their repertoire of behaviours, relationships, and work practices.

You'll notice that I refer to the change of mindset and behaviours as being both practised (at least at the start) and authentic. How is this possible? Surely a changed version of ourselves that needs practice and rehearsal is unlikely to be the authentic self that comes naturally to us and requires little effort? Surely, we need to be true to ourselves and not pretend to be someone that we're not? I completely agree. When we are changing our habits, we are not, in my mind, pretending to be someone else, but if we recognise that change is needed, and we set ourselves an authentic goal for achieving some new habits, then all the effort and experimentation will be in service of achieving these authentic goals, which, I believe, makes the new mindset and behaviours both practised and authentic.

The ability to shift our mindset authentically in relation to a given context helps in other ways when we are trying to change our habits. A few years ago, I was introduced to the work of Charles Duhigg, who has conducted research into how habits work, and he has devised a framework to encourage us to look at how we might change or reshape any of our current habits. Developed from studies by the Massachusetts Institute of Technology (MIT), Duhigg shows that there are three parts at the core of every habit which loop around to reinforce our customs and practices.

The three parts are the habit itself, which could be a shadow habit we are trying to lose or a golden habit we are trying to learn. On either side of this, there is the cue or trigger that starts the habit and then the positive reward or consequence we get from the habit that will sustain it. This progression from the trigger to the habit and to the reward provides us with rich territory to explore when we are motivated to change any of our behavioural habits.

As we realise the need for change and become ready to transform, it's helpful to consider what are the cues that trigger any shadow behaviours and habits that we want to alter, and what are the rewards you get from behaving in this way. For example, are your shadow behaviours triggered especially when you are tired, or by the apparent thoughtlessness of others, or by certain behaviours, personality types, or language? Becoming more aware of these triggers matters in the process of behavioural change.

Similarly, being honest with yourself about the 'rewards' you get from exercising your shadow behaviours is an important conversation to have with yourself, or with others, about yourself. Knowing that you are using behaviours that enable you to get your own way, to hurt others who have hurt you, or to shift blame to avoid taking responsibility for yourself is a vital part of the journey of change. Because of this, it is very important that we bring compassion for ourselves into these conversations and that we see these 'rewards' as part of the human condition. Do these shadow responses make us 'bad' people behaving badly or 'typical' people who have yet to find golden responses to what triggers us? These links between what triggers us, our subsequent habits, and the 'rewards' that we get from behaving in this way provide us with more helpful strategies to enable us to change our habits.

For example, once we understand more clearly what is triggering our shadow behaviours, we can work on developing an alternative narrative about that trigger. Going back to the model of mind, body, and voice, this change of narrative is a mindset shift about this trigger. Where we had previously interpreted the behaviour of someone else in one way, can we find an alternative interpretation?

One simple example of this is clear in my coaching work with candidates before promotion interviews, where I provide them with the opportunity to prepare for being on the receiving end of interview questions (a very specific type of trigger). What is very noticeable in this context is how the candidate's behaviour is visibly influenced by any negative mindset about the interview; for example, that the interviewer is 'trying to catch me out' with their questions. The belief that, at least during the interview, the interviewer will look for a weakness or flaw in the candidate's case for promotion creates responses that appear guarded or defensive and rarely enable the candidate to be at their best.

However, once the interviewee can put themselves in the shoes of the interviewer and empathise with their need to interview with appropriate rigour, the candidate can prepare with an expectation that there might be some questions for which they don't have a ready answer and, out of this, they can prepare some helpful strategies for what they will do if this happens. The mindset shift from 'they're trying to catch me out' to 'I expect not to have ready answers for everything, and I've got a strategy for dealing with that' changes the nature of the trigger which gives access to behaviours and responses that were previously disabled.

Alternatively, if a candidate has had a series of 'tough' interviews and their confidence is low, it is sometimes harder to shift any negative mindset and, in this case, without changing any interpretation of that trigger, the candidate can still practise and learn an alternative set of responses. In this way, we start with a behavioural change before the shift in mindset. And as the candidate 'appears' to be more authentic and confident in the interview, they start to feel more positive about the experience and, over time, the behavioural change can lead to a shift in mindset.

As I have mentioned previously, if we want to make any behavioural change habitual, the sequence of trigger, habit, and reward should also encourage us to clarify the rewards we are getting from any of these changes. When we are developing golden habits, the rewards we gain from this are important if we think of them in terms of the positive outcome of the new habit or routine we have created. Rewards can be extrinsic (external / tangible / visible) and/or intrinsic (internal / felt / experienced), and you can create short-term or longer-term rewards.

In my coaching sessions with interview candidates, I am keen to offer genuine praise and appreciation (an extrinsic reward) for any helpful change of behaviour, as well as explore where the candidate is feeling easier, happier, more relaxed and confident (intrinsic rewards) because of their efforts. Of course, a good outcome in the subsequent interview is the ultimate extrinsic reward for any successful change of habits in this context.

This exploration of how we get rewarded for our existing habits is also, I believe, a way to begin the work we can do with others who are still unaware of, or resistant to, the need for change. If part of your job is to manage someone who is exhibiting shadow behaviours and habits, and the person has, to date, shown no signs of the need to change, you may have to begin the process by which you clearly articulate the negative consequences to the individual if these shadow behaviours persist. Of course, this is not about you adopting threatening and bullying behaviour yourself but acting with kindness and compassion for the individual, you can be assertive and clear about what is in it for them (the incentives and positive rewards) to change their behaviours, and the risks to them (the negative consequences) for continuing with their shadow behaviours.

In these conversations, it can also sometimes be very helpful to understand fully and deeply and have compassion and empathy for what is currently rewarding those individuals who are using shadow behaviours. If it is part of the human condition to be self-interested and self-serving at times, let's not be surprised if our shadow behaviours bring us 'rewards' that serve us but are detrimental to others. It is very easy to be critical of these behaviours, but if we can show our understanding of why someone might behave in this way, it's helpful to recognise this whilst providing clarity about the negative consequences to the individual of not changing their behaviours.

An obvious example of this is the shadow behaviours of persistent lateness, half-finished work, leaving work early, or a lack of effort in completing tasks. These individuals, who could be choosing to work on their own terms rather than complying with the norms or requirements of the team or organisation, are often criticised as being selfish or lazy. Of course, this will be at odds with the individual's own experience of their behaviours, as they will likely find significant rewards by working in this way.

So, in managing these types of behaviours, we're unlikely to get much engagement from the individual if we begin by criticising them for being selfish and lazy. If, instead, we empathise with their need to do the work on their own terms and try to understand their motivation for behaving in these ways, then we can work with them to find a good solution that is acceptable to all concerned and will allow them to meet their obligations to the organisation. Empathising with the individual and being clear and assertive about the issue is sometimes called 'tough love' and this can be a very helpful strategy in assisting individuals to change their habits if they are currently unaware of the need to change.

I began by explaining where my own personal journey began into the exploration of how humans can consciously and authentically change their behaviours and habits to achieve different outcomes. It began in the rehearsal rooms of my drama school and, decades later, it continues in my leadership development work and coaching with individuals who are, inevitably, at different stages of their readiness for change. Although my journey in this exploration will always be a work in progress, I am encouraged by my observations that humans are all capable of change and that those who are most successful in changing their habits are, commonly, adopting at least some of the following strategies:

- Empathise with yourself and others who are yet to understand the need to change and be honest with yourself and others about the potential risks of not changing
- Clarify the cues and triggers for any shadow behaviours and explore ways of adapting, reshaping, rethinking, or removing these triggers
- Where the triggers persist, practise, and rehearse new responses that will break the patterns of your current responses
- Create authentic goals so that your practice and rehearsals result in authentic outcomes
- Enjoy, celebrate, savour, and relish your successes and the intrinsic and extrinsic rewards that derive from the habits you change.

Collaboration and cooperation
Johan Schaar

A vital part of healthy leadership and organisations is to ensure that leadership is conducted in a collaborative, purpose-focused and value-based manner. This acts as a beacon for others and often leads to the construction and maintenance of a supportive work culture.

Johan Schaar is a very experienced leader in the humanitarian world and has worked with dignity, respect, humility, and considerateness in a variety of complex settings where it was essential to build collaboration and cooperation. Here, we listen to Johan's perspectives on his approach to leadership and the importance of collaboration and cooperation.

My background and leadership qualities

I worked in research and, when I had completed my doctoral dissertation, I left to work for the Red Cross. This meant that I could enter a field that had always engaged me and, coincidentally, I found that my training as a researcher became an asset in the humanitarian sector and other work that I have since had. This was the most deliberate and thought through step I took in my career.

Subsequently, there were many coincidences in my long and winding career. When opportunities arose, I mostly said 'yes' even though there was an element of risk, as I did not always know exactly what I would be doing. I have since worked in development, the environment, climate change including associated security implications; and for governments, voluntary organisations, and think tanks.

It is important to take seriously the role of a leader, understand it, and realise that it places special requirements on you to personify the values of the organisation. You need to be polite, set an example and give space to your team, recognising and valuing each person and their contribution.

To embody values, you need to be prepared to take good risks (without being reckless) and not be too passive or defensive. You don't need to change your personality, but you use your abilities and adapt. I am essentially an introverted person and I recognise that by trying to be more communicative.

Leadership qualities for cooperation and collaboration

Given my preference for working alone, I balance that tendency when leading a team with collaboration in mind. Showing that collaboration and coordination are vital is the first step, helping the team understand they are necessary for the work and to take the situation into account. As a leader, you need to introduce mechanisms such as cross-functional work to promote and exploit the function of collaboration. This often leads to enrichment of the quality of the collectively done work. People should also be recognised for their unique experience while acknowledging that the team is more than the sum of its parts. By working in mixed teams, people are also getting to know themselves and each other slightly differently than if they worked alone.

Recognising what has already been done and achieved as well as focusing on learning will help. These are key facets which are not always taken seriously in organisations, especially when there is a relatively high staff turnover and the use of short-term contracts, as in the humanitarian sector. Additionally, we need to learn about and value, more, the respective institutional memories.

Looking for opportunities can be enjoyable. For example, finding possibilities for collaboration with those who may not be immediately recognised as needed for the work but have other mandates, roles, and therefore perspectives that can enrich your own, more limited one. This can lead to increased value for the team and the work.

It is also important to work with other parts of the infrastructure cooperatively. Actions are more likely to be taken for an effective result. Being prepared to give and take is integral to taking part in a coordination mechanism; leveraging pressure points, by recognising what others have that you may not, also helps. Being willing to go the extra mile can lead to better outcomes, which may not occur if the team just focuses on the tasks in a narrower way, i.e. it provides a wider perspective.

As a leader, you may not always be able to select who will be in your team. Thus being willing to work with who is present is imperative, as is the need to understand that group dynamics will shift as people leave and join the team.

It is essential to provide space for reflection (yourself and others) and for this to be taken seriously. Doing so will allow you to think about what you are doing, as an individual or in groups. You will internalise the importance of what you have been doing and reach conclusions so that you can use those insights. (It should not become a mechanical activity.) This embeds learning and contributes to remembering, the institutional memory, and prevents the amnesia that often happens in our high turnover, rapid and crisis-oriented humanitarian sector.

Being willing, as a leader, to be challenged, especially in your failures, is necessary. Asking subordinates for their perspectives in such situations allows you to use the learning and experience you have experienced. Of course, this needs to be done honestly and kindly. For this to happen, subordinates need to know that they will not be sanctioned for speaking. When you permit such interactions, then this indicates generosity in being open.

Possible difficulties

If there is conflict, it is essential to recognise whether addressing the issue is part of your scope of influence. If this is the case, then it is an opportunity to deal with the matter.

There is, sometimes, scepticism or questioning by stakeholders, especially if they feel that their role and responsibilities are the most important. Helping people recognise we need all parts for the entire project to function is a place to start and think about hope for the success of the project. Encourage them to remember the higher purpose and that understanding each other's perspective is necessary.

Think about what could undermine collaboration, e.g. if anyone is cynical, this can be problematic as it may adversely affect others. Working out in advance and building defences against the possible lack of collaboration is important, especially in the early stages. This is very essential in high-risk environments. This includes recognising that team members will have different backgrounds and perspectives, such as if they are national or international. These can be very helpful to the greater task but can sometimes be an issue, e.g. disparities in income and privileges.

A role for competitive behaviour in collaboration and cooperation?

The humanitarian sector is very competitive—for funds, jobs, positions, and so forth. Competition is needed in a team so that people perform at their very best. The organisation needs it as well as the fact that the assigned work requires it. However, group dynamics may lead to some tension if competitive behaviour is used, e.g. colleagues thinking that someone is just trying to advance their career.

Hopes for the future of collaboration through leadership

'Events at the time of writing (withdrawal of US Armed Forces from Afghanistan (August 2021)) remind me (Johan) of the crucial importance of learning from what is happening for better protection for staff and so that it will not occur again.' Localisation and devolved delegation from headquarters to the local level will mean that the often extreme distances between where decisions are made and where people must live with the consequences will be avoided and therefore, hopefully, there will be better outcomes.

Chapter Six

Readiness For Change—Interventions

Change is extremely difficult, even when we consider we are ready. 'I was responsible for ensuring that a staff restaurant was established in a village near to a town in a poor country. I found a restaurateur in the nearby town who was willing to open a staff café, which he then did. The food was good, and staff wanted more on the menu.

I am interested in cooking and asked the restaurateur if I could help. He agreed; I went to observe his employees cook in the kitchen and later discussed the menu with him. I suggested I could help by showing them how to make an omelette in the traditional style, a beef burger, and a fish stew.

He was a polite, kind man and he invited me to work with his employees who were very welcoming. I showed them how to make a filled omelette in the traditional manner as they used to put oil in the frying pan, add cut vegetables, break two eggs into the pan and then stir with a spoon until the eggs solidified. I also showed them how to make a beef burger using local flat bread and, finally, fish stew. They all politely thanked me, and I went away thinking that I had been a great success.

When I returned the next month, I saw that the burgers were a hit and even selling in his restaurant in the town; the fish recipe had been adapted. However, they had gone back to their own way of making an omelette. The only difference was how they used the spoon. Instead of stirring with it, they moved it from side to side as you would with a fork. (Rightly, they could have interpreted my efforts as an imposition.)'

This story tells us that people change and adopt new habits and ideas when they fit in and are useful. Otherwise, they are likely to change only a little or not at all because the habit is not deemed important enough to adopt. Therefore, it is important to think about how and why people change a little more before we move onto considering interventions at any level.

The path of change (individual and organisational)

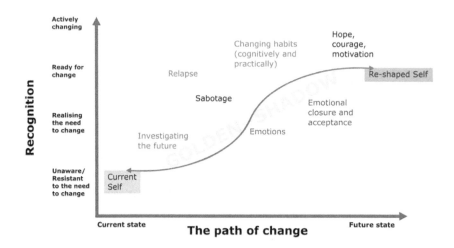

Although the diagram above is linear, change is not. There are many factors that are involved. The diagram is inspired by the work of Dick Beckhard (whose life is discussed in Chapter Five), William Bridges, Elizabeth Kubler Ross, James Prochaska, and Carlo Di Clemente.

The voyage from the current Self to the re-shaped Self is rarely smooth and in one direction. It often meanders. Thus, we have separated out the practical from the emotional and cognitive and have assumed that change is not at all unidirectional and the path taken depends on the readiness of the person or organisation. Some will, regardless of readiness, want to start at different stages. For example, your colleagues may want to explore emotions and then think about which habits need altering. You may want to spend a lot of time first investigating the future.

Readiness for change is an important factor. Going through the change process is much easier if you are already on the path to realistically accepting the need for the change. You are more likely to let go emotionally of your existing life frame, keep what works and create new habits, and progress through closure and acceptance to your new life frame. It means that you are ready and willing to consider future options even though you cannot visualise them.

If a person is essentially unaware or in denial of the need for change, even after a thorough analysis, then they are extremely unlikely to go through the change process healthily. They may even resort to sabotage or just not take real action.

It is worth stopping to think about how you have changed in the past and map it onto the diagram so you can learn about how you are likely to change now. What was golden and shadow about how you altered?

The diagram above also applies to organisational change. The only difference is that there are, usually, many more people involved and so they may be at different stages of accepting change and may prefer different paths. Given this, it is vital to recognise how the organisation has changed in the past and how different colleagues are likely to progress through change or not.

An explanation of the diagram

The vertical axis describes the stages that a person or organisation can go through when change appears in their life. Some move through change easily and adapt smoothly with few hiccups. These will be the people and colleagues who attend all the change planning meetings and think about what could be different.

Others will be in denial. 'In my younger days, I did not like change, and this was well known by people close to me. Once, I ignored a health problem. Everyone could see that I was unwell, and they knew I would not be prepared to listen. My partner, understanding this, waited until I was too tired to argue, told me he was very concerned about my health and that he would like me to get professional help. I was so tired, just wanting to sleep, that I agreed mainly because I craved rest.'

Others may be reluctant throughout the process and then all you can expect from them is the new range of habits and behaviours. Someone could say, 'I don't know what all the fuss is about, I am doing the same thing as I was even though my job title has changed.'

Some people take time to adjust. For example, 'I was involved in a de-institutionalisation programme for a hospital for people with differences and one of the staff I worked with was passionately against the move to ordinary housing in the community. She argued vehemently against our ideas throughout the planning process, even though she took part in the change. Six months after the house opened, and the people had moved in, I met her at a barbecue at the house and she wanted to know why we had not done this sooner…'

Self (individual and organisational)

Changes start with looking at the current sense of Self (as a person or as a group) and working out what is viable and helpful and what may need adjusting. This includes all aspects of the Self as it steers and coordinates us in life and work. If we progress through the change process, then we will give ourselves permission to re-shape our Selves and be prepared to listen and move to the future. This will include all the elements in the diagram, including letting go, having closure, and cleansing emotions. Most important is the need to look at the complete Self, including positive and negative aspects. It may also be worth thinking about the linkages between your current and future Self.

Investigating the future

We may have been given a glimpse of the future through a refined mission statement or by accepting a new job, retiring, or moving to a new house. While we cannot accurately predict every part of the future, we can investigate by asking questions about it. For example, we could learn about the new organisational structure, find out about the new company, attend seminars about retirement, or visit the new town. The investigation can give us a new sense of comfort in what is an uncertain time by helping us face and imagine the future.

Emotions

Some models imply that there is a sequence to the emotions that people experience during change. However, most people encounter a myriad of emotions and shift from one to the other, sometimes in the space of an hour. This is a time when we are often confused, feel uncomfortable and look for something or someone to ground us. Emotions can also include happiness, sadness, grief, acceptance, joy, anger, and jealousy amongst others.

The most important thing about emotions is to allow them their expression (when appropriate), acknowledge them, and use the positive ones to energise, while letting go of the negative ones. Suppression, in our experience, has never worked. Eventually, the suppressed emotions seep through, often unhealthily, e.g. biting your nails, sudden and unexplained anger outbursts.

A way of letting go of emotions is to think about them, why you feel them, and where (in your body) you experience them. Think about what is needed to let go of the undesirable ones, e.g. forgiving yourself or someone else. Write all of this down and, if you feel comfortable enough to let go, destroy the paper and think of a positive feeling instead.

A surfeit of emotions can also make us feel uncomfortable. Think about what will help you feel grounded during this period. For example, remembering someone who helps/helped you feel strong and comforted. 'I remember my father and grandfather at such times.'

Sabotage

Given that we, as human beings, are imperfect, inevitably, we may sabotage ourselves or the change process. This is more likely to happen if we are not ready for the change. An organisation was going to close its factory and move to a new site where the buildings were more spread out. The managers described the new site to the staff and had photos of each work area with the names of those who would use that space underneath. However, staff did not want to move to the new place. Every night, someone would remove the photos and every morning, a new set of photos would be put up by the managers on the walls of the project room.

High levels of stress can also lead to people sabotaging themselves either individually or at the organisational level. Something, we are not sure what, happens when people are too stressed, and the wrong choice is then made. For example, despite being told that a virtual planning meeting would be held on Microsoft Teams, a very anxious group uses Zoom and then complains when the meeting does not start on time.

Emotional closure and acceptance

For us to change, we need to let go emotionally and release ourselves. Hanging on to past emotions and feelings can keep us in the past. Sometimes, taking time or creating a brief ceremony of letting go will help and give us closure and acceptance. You could organise an event that marks the end of one part of life and celebrates the start of the next element.

Relapse

This is inevitable, and we can be unaware of it. Relapse often occurs when we are feeling uncertain and want to return to what was comfortable and known, e.g. going to someone's old office after they have moved, referring to an old policy because you prefer it.

It is worth, at the beginning of the change process, stopping and thinking about how you could relapse and what you can do to recognise the warning signs and then recover and continue as before.

Changing habits (cognitively and practically)

Of all the various elements of the path of change, this is, perhaps, the element that has the greatest potential to affect others. By shifting our previously held beliefs and attitudes and by changing our habitual behaviours and strategies can often be a powerful signal to others that we are committed to change. And a conscious change in behaviour is, perhaps, the most visible manifestation that a change has occurred.

As we have explored elsewhere, unless we realise the need to change, it is extremely challenging to find the energy and motivation to alter our habits. Challenging, but not impossible, as we explored in Chapter Five with Jamie Ripman. Even when we are ready for change, unhelpful and shadow thoughts, emotions, and behaviours can be so embedded and habitual that they are difficult to shift. However, once we awaken to the need to change, there is practical work that can be done that enables us to move into new ways of being, feeling, sounding, and behaving that can be discovered, rehearsed, practised, and embedded so that we emerge from this process with new, authentic, sustainable, and golden habits.

In Chapter Five, we considered this further with an expert perspective from one of our contributors, Jamie Ripman, who began professional life in the performing arts before moving into the field of leadership development. We're not arguing that changing a habit is about giving an Oscar-winning performance, but sustained behavioural change often starts with a conscious shift of language, vocal tone, gesture, physical or vocal energy and in this respect, we are, perhaps, beginning with an experimental, performed version of ourselves as we embark on a journey towards sustained and authentic change.

Hope, courage, and motivation

It takes these three qualities to give yourself permission to travel on the path of change and especially towards the end of the journey. If they are present in abundance, then it is likely that you will change as required. If one is missing or not present in sufficient quantities, then the path may be more arduous and difficult. At the very least, courage and motivation should be present in sufficient amounts, and this can often be done by deciding to be accompanied by others who will reinforce your hope and courage and then motivate you and themselves.

The exercise

Please use the diagram to explore how you (individually or collectively) have changed in the past and think about what your learning has been. Then, consider each element for the current change and reflect on the key aspects.

Where were you in terms of recognising the need to change? Which version of your Self was the starting point? What was the journey taken? What was the emergent and re-shaped Self at the end of the journey?

The learning is...

Chapter Seven

Building The Golden And Positive For Overall Healthiness

Hopefully, having carried out your analysis (individual or collective), you will have achieved a greater sense of awareness of the issues, the factors that help or hinder, and how the golden and shadow are involved. You will also, by now, know how ready you are to change and what the change pattern is likely to be. Think about what you have learned from the assessments, what needs to continue and is golden, and what needs to be addressed.

It is now time to consider what you want as an intervention. Are you ready to break the sound barrier or are you more inclined to shift only a little towards the future? Remember we move towards our futures in different ways. Some will move at warp speed. They could include new actions but then may go back a little, occasionally, to what they knew and were comfortable with. Some may not feel strong enough to work towards the future or they may have a different perspective to others. After independence in India, Mahatma Gandhi wanted an economic model that focussed on household production, whereas Pandit Nehru chose one that was much more traditional—rapid industrialisation.

The aim of this section is to provide you with a wide range of interventions from which you can choose to address your issues and move towards a healthier you. They will help you build on what you have learned and re-shape your Self (individual or collective) so that you can coordinate and function in a more balanced way.

We are using the concept of **overall healthiness** incorporating living with the shadow side. All the elements are interrelated and codependent.

The key aspects of **overall healthiness** are:

Self, compassion, and respect
Well-being, mental health, and physical health
Emotions, cognitions, physical (body), and relationships
Synergy with purpose and values
Material resources and the environment
Diversity
Living with the shadow side
Administrative issues
Leadership and organisational interventions

One element without the others is usually not sufficient to become a healthier leader or organisation. But please remember to choose what is vital, doable, and will challenge and stretch you. Easy for us to say, we know. Please also make your interventions practical and behavioural.

Pause for a few moments to honour history and its role in your present and future. What needs to be brought forward and what needs to be left behind?

All our recommendations below can be adapted for use as a leader or organisation.

A. Self, compassion, and respect

In our models, we argue that the Self is core and has a coordinating function for us as individuals or organisations. It is therefore very crucial that the sense of Self is inculcated with compassion and respect as fundamental facets. In this section, we help you consider your sense of Self in relation to compassion and respect. However, please remember that Self also has a link to the other aspects we mention below.

Compassion has been growing in popularity as a concept and intervention in leadership and organisations. Some of this is linked to the increasing awareness and knowledge of Buddhist practices and principles. The Dalai Lama describes compassion as a 'natural human quality'.

We can ponder why it is a vital part of life and work and that will take another book.

Briefly, some argue that this is the next phase of the life of the world where we become more compassionate to and considerate of each other, i.e. the Age of Aquarius. The Hopi, First Nation of America, call it the entrance of the World of the Fifth Hoop. The most important thing is to accept that we have acknowledged its importance and then think about how we can bring it more into our work and lives as leaders and organisations.

For true healing, compassion needs to be brought into the centre of the person or the organisation and not as an add-on. A webinar on compassion and leadership will make participants think about how to be more considerate for the duration of the session, and that may be all. There needs to be a wholesale incorporation of compassion into all relevant aspects.

Compassion without true respect can lead to selfishness and mere sympathy. Compassion, aligned with regard for the other person, means that you will be truly compassionate with anyone you interact with. This means that you shift from giving and making yourself feel better to sharing and supporting with dignity.

Look back at the analyses that you have done as part of reading this book. What have you learned about your approach to compassion and respect?

The learning..

Here are some suggestions to consider as interventions at the individual or organisational level.

Building compassion

Make time to include and think about compassion in your life. You could start a contemplative practice if you have not already done so. Here are some possibilities.

> Create a time during your day to think about being compassionate. Write about those moments when you have shown compassion. How did the recipient feel? Think about when others showed you compassion. How did you feel?

> Choose a picture or memory that depicts compassion for you. Sit quietly and calmly and slow down your breathing. As it slows down, clear your mind and dismiss any stray thoughts that appear. Now, in silence, focus on the picture or memory for five minutes. Then think about how this practice shifted your thinking, feelings, and body.

Deliberate about a sentence that helps you think of being compassionate. Here is one:

'We should, each of us, in all our choices, aim to produce the greatest
happiness we can and especially the least misery.'
Richard Layard

Now write an essay to yourself about what this means to you in your life. Store the essay and return it to regularly to remind yourself.

Sometimes it helps to think of compassion alongside sadness and hardship.

Consider these questions:

What can I do to become more compassionate to myself, others, and the world?
How can I help myself, others, and the world to address the sadness that is present?

Perhaps think about something you have seen and experienced. 'I was being driven through a very large refugee camp once and, in passing, saw a little boy running and playing. He had one toy. It was an empty plastic bottle that someone had cut a hole in, so it could resemble a ship or car, and tied a string to it so that the child could play with it.

The little boy was running and dragging the toy behind him, and he was smiling and why wouldn't he? This memory reminds me of the importance of care and compassion, even in difficult circumstances. And of how much I had compared to that family.'

Openness to the future

What can you do to ensure that you remain compassionate, flexible and open to the future? Perhaps you could allocate some time each day to pause, clear your mind, time and heart and just listen. What will you do to make sure that this time is honoured regularly?

Using these and other practices is very important to open ourselves up to the compassion that is already within us significantly. It is important that these are regular practices and not just occasionally used.

How can these become part of daily practice, either as a single person or as a team or as an organisation? Could you, as suggested by Monica Worline, create compassion-oriented groups where people meet to discuss how to be compassionate in as many parts of the organisation as possible. How can it become an integral part of key work practices such as meetings, supervision, and appraisals?

Enhancing respect

The more senior we become, the more difficult it can be to respect one and all. And yet there is much to learn from people we usually ignore. 'Raba was the cleaner for our offices. He was part of a contracted-out service and earned little. Regardless, he came in early and made sure our offices were exemplary in terms of cleanliness. Some saw a poor man doing a menial job, but we knew how professional he was. He would diligently clean the rust off his brooms and make sure that all of his cleaning equipment was functional.'

We can be nice without respecting the person, perhaps because they are not as qualified as we are. Why not stop and think about how much respect you have for the others in your life? How are the least senior people treated? How do you show respect? What more could you do?

LaGree et al. (2021) found that employees emphasised the importance of being valued and respected by managers and colleagues. It was a major contributor to their ability to adapt at work and deal with problems.

Equally, it is important to have self-respect. If we do not, then we are very unlikely to respect others positively. It is worth checking to see how much respect you give yourself. Is it sufficient? What is the evidence that you truly respect yourself? For example, do you choose actions that benefit others at your own expense? What can you do to build your self-respect?

Compassion and respect in teams

Daniel Goleman describes emotional intelligence as having four key components. For teams and organisations, he recommends we need the following to embed compassion and emotional intelligence in organisations.

Increasing interpersonal understanding is key and leads to good empathy between team members so that they know and understand each other's strengths and skills, e.g. knowing who prefers working in the early morning, identifying who is better at art and creativity and who is excellent at using technology. All this also decreases stress levels. A team can achieve this by providing opportunities for informal discussions and sometimes specifically discussing how to support each other.

Team Self and group evaluation with increasing awareness is another factor to be encouraged. This should also become a regular practice by asking questions such as: 'In the past month, what were our successes and areas for learning? How was our level of self-respect and respect? What praise can we give each other? What were our Velcro (sticky) moments and how can we grow?' You could also ask the team to be creative and make items or drawings that depict their answers to the questions.

Being able to be truthful is a rare and vital commodity and one that is not always present in teams and organisations. People need to feel comfortable in their home and work environments so that they can tell the truth. You can encourage this by setting an example, by allowing people to speak freely but with respect. Once this is established as a practice, it will grow and shape conversations so that issues can be discussed more fully.

Meaningful accountability needs to be part of a compassionate team. Collective ownership and responsibility also need to be encouraged so that people feel they are part of a greater mission.

Another important quality is the ability to listen well, without judgement. The desired state is to relax, and listen openly and silently while non-verbally acknowledging the person. Listening intently also includes waiting until the person has finished speaking before working out what to say. This means that the listener must trust themselves enough to know that they will utter an appropriate response.

Work practices, policies, and procedures also need to be inclusive of compassion with respect. Talking about being compassionate does not matter if you refuse to let staff work less than ten hours a day or insist on them calling you Madam or Sir. Why not let staff review their work practices to see what is effective and supportive and what is not? The King's Fund in England highlights the importance of encouraging autonomy, belonging, and contribution.

How many of your policies and procedures, beyond the existence of a code of conduct, encourage people to be autonomous, positive, helpful, compassionate, and kind? Why not try to develop and simplify existing ones so that they encourage the golden and provide guidance on how to address shadow behaviours?

A practice that encourages time for self-compassion and self-care is vital in the organisational culture and structure. Why not ensure that this becomes part of the annual goals for individuals and teams?

A compassionate and respectful relationship between the team, organisation, and the wider world is also needed. This may mean that some will have to address or, at least, be honest about their purpose. We now speak about stakeholder capitalism, the Triple Bottom Line, or ESG (Environmental, Social, Governance) but how are these compassionate for all citizens when there is a profit motive embedded in them? If the decision is to be profit oriented, then it is important to be honest about this and adopt the principle of doing as little harm as possible.

Ideally, the leader, team and organisation should be compassionate and work to do no harm to any person or the planet. We explore these facets in more detail below. We all have a collective responsibility to contribute to healing the world, and the climate. Otherwise, if we do not, we will leave a diminished future for the next generation.

If all the above become part of a team or organisation, then people are more willing to stay. The work environment improves, trust increases, and performance and compassionate behaviours become the norm for human interaction. People feel cared for and part of a greater purpose.

Match the intention with thoughts and actions

Having good intentions is not enough. We must turn them into thoughts and actions. First, consider the extent to which you include and use emotional intelligence.

Make sure that you remain self-aware of how compassionate and respectful you are as an individual and organisation. Ask for regular feedback so that you do not become complacent.

Check that you are regulating yourself in terms of your energy, motivation, emotions, and courage. Try to have as positive an approach as possible. Think about how you can move forward instead of worrying about what may go wrong.

Attempt to be open and aware at the social, personal, and organisational level. This can often happen by just ensuring that you are breathing properly, emptying your thoughts, and then sensing the surrounding environment. James and Arroba (2005) consider 'reading' a vital political skill alongside 'carrying'/being ethical. Their definition of reading is the ability to sense and understand the inner working of others and organisations: how people interact, decision making, overt and covert agendas, formal and informal leadership, and politics. Carrying refers to the preference (or not) to act with integrity or its opposite.

Finally, it is important to have some skills in relationship management. This means having a wide repertoire of behaviours including knowing how to influence, coach and mentor, manage conflicts, and inspire and support the team to work.

On a personal level, compassion with respect requires that you find ways of building and maintaining your own self-confidence and worth. For example, by praising yourself now and again, or carrying a memento that reminds you of someone important in your life and who is confident. Find ways to be kind to yourself and others, even if it is a simple greeting.

Vitally, it is important to make time for self-awareness and compassion. Why not book some time for yourself, perhaps switching off all the technology for a weekend, making sure that someone else is available to provide help if necessary?

If someone comes to you with a problem, don't immediately generate a solution (which you probably can) but help the person, via open Socratic questions, to investigate the issue and find their own solution. Review work with the person so that supervision becomes a regular learning opportunity, more than a discussion about whether they have achieved a target. In contrast, apparently, an institution used to ask employees to achieve eight goals a week because eight rhymes with the word great.

Making time to learn from others can also be refreshing if it is done honourably. There are some leadership programmes that, in our experience, have taken participants to visit poor people and the sole aim seemed to be making the participants increase their sense of global responsibility. The people who were visited rarely got anything from the discussion and, sometimes, were not even paid for their time.

At the organisational level, it is important to think about how you can involve and engage others in the designing of any change plans. If you do this, then people are more likely to help you follow through with the plan. Ideally they should already be engaged but if not, then you could invite them to participate. Sometimes it is worth starting with the most willing and then let the news of their efforts spread to and encourage others. It is said that you need about 30% of staff on board to effect change.

It is now time to choose your actions and behaviours to bring into reality your intention for Self, compassion, and respect.

Based on your reading of the above, how would you describe your future sense of Self (Individual or organisational)?

Which behaviours do you want to use to encourage greater compassion and respect, e.g. asking people to set aside ten minutes at the start of the day to reflect on compassion and respect and how they will show it in their work, making time to praise yourself and colleagues?

1.
2.
3.
4.

What cues and triggers are needed to embed the behaviours in daily practice, e.g. setting an alarm reminding you to be contemplative, asking someone to check in with you about your progress? Remember, it takes 30 days for a new habit to embed itself in people's repertoire and so you may need to be patient.

B. Well-being, mental health and physical health

Like compassion, well-being, mental health, and physical health have become very popular interventions in most sectors, especially during the COVID pandemic. Most well-being programmes will have a range of components: stress management, self-care, opportunities to learn about mindfulness, yoga, regular health checks, exercise, etc.

It is also worth noting that there is usually only a limited uptake of mental health and well-being programmes. Valencia (2021) reports that Gartner survey results indicated that although 87% of respondents had access to such services, only 23% used them, partly because of associated stigmas.

Organisations can ignore the importance of recognising that there is a continuum from well-being to mental health problems to mental illness. Business (regardless of sector), especially now, must consider how to support people at all points of their mental health or illness and address the stigmas that occur. This is important now because living through the COVID pandemic led to an increase in problems such as anxiety and depression and to most people being more vulnerable in terms of their mental health. It will take time for people to recover psychologically from the impact of living through COVID.

Interventions to promote mental health could help managers and colleagues become more willing to discuss such sensitive matters, supporting each other to recognise when someone may need help. If someone becomes mentally ill, then the organisation has a responsibility to ensure that they have a good return to work. Some have ensured that this occurs in their institutions.

Similarly, individuals and organisations need to ensure that physical health is looked after. This can be done by going to the gym and exercising regularly, but also by the organisation ensuring that people work sensibly.

If you look at the research on well-being, psychosocial, and health risk, then there are other organisational interventions that are also necessary for good health: noble leaders who have and use their competencies, team structures that are clear, defined roles, good interpersonal supports alongside sufficient resources, knowledge and use of good self-care and stress management approaches. A suitable home and work-life balance, access to mental health and physical health services and support if working directly with vulnerable groups are all important. Most of these factors fall into the category of ensuring that people's mental and physical health are, at least, maintained as well as trying to provide a healthy physical work environment.

Equally, organisations need to look at their policies and procedures to make sure that they are promoting wellness and supporting people when they are in need, either daily or when they go into crisis. Some organisations now do not record sick leave; staff may take it as needed. The Detroit Library system has monthly focus days where staff can use the opportunity to stop and reflect on how they have been working and change what is needed. Others create well-being support groups in which staff volunteers (sometimes with professional support) can help each other. For example, by sharing how they are feeling, offering well-being activities to each other—these can involve learning to cook, languages, or simply just having fun.

C. Emotions, cognitions, physical (body), and relationships

If a person's mental health, well-being, and physical health are in synchrony, then their emotions, cognitions, relationships, and their bodies will also be working for them as opposed to against them. As individuals, we therefore have an extra obligation to do our utmost to look after ourselves using some of the approaches described here. As organisations, there is similarly a collective responsibility to ensure that people feel centred, relaxed, and well enough to look after themselves and each other.

The quality of current relationships will depend on the extent to which we are reinforcing the golden or the shadow side of ourselves. It is worth carrying out an audit to see who is helping you become the best of you and who is not. Then you can decide, either as an individual or a group, what you want to do about the relationships while considering your hopes for your future Self.

D. Synergy with purpose and values

As important as well-being, mental health, and physical health are, there are other vital facets. We all not only need a sense of purpose but also the opportunity to express this in our life and work. Some of us do live our purpose and intention, but this is rare, even in the humanitarian sector. For complete healthiness, we need to look for places and work that allow us to live our purpose. If this cannot be, then we need to accept, compromise, and acknowledge the difficulties that then arise.

Purpose, ideally, needs to be underpinned by values, including integrity. Having a clear set of values ensures that the purpose has a solid foundation and can be enacted. Being an individual or organisation that has purpose and integrity will lead to greater respect, both internally and externally.

Organisations, regardless of sector (public, private, not-for profit, humanitarian), can help people live their purpose in synergy with the corporate purpose more than they do. At the very least, organisations can acknowledge the dilemma that comes when there is a mismatch between personal and corporate purpose. This can start with honest discussions with staff.

For example, it may be useful, both personally and collectively, to look at the work and behaviours that are present and find ways of reconciling what is real versus what you hope for. Think back to what you have learned about your purpose/mission (individual and collective). Look at the work and behaviours that are used to express purpose. Then fit them into one of these three categories:

Mission central
Mission neutral
Just there to make money.

(These categories were what Dick Beckhard suggested to judge the work that the Office for Public Management (OPM) in England was asked to do. He advised it was best to hope for the first two categories but also be prepared for the third. This was a good mnemonic to hold on to as the strapline for OPM was 'managing for social result' (alongside striving for financial probity).)

Then, find a way of either learning to live with the reality or bring more meaning to your work honestly. Some use a process called job crafting and, while this can be helpful, it is important to make sure that the changes to someone's work have value and are respectful.

Organisations could do more to align their structures and jobs so that people blend their purpose with that of the organisation. We often wonder what would happen if organisations investigated the extent to which their cultures and feelings of employees matched and enabled their purpose. 'When I worked in the National Health Service in England, where presumably there should have been a close match between personal and professional purpose, I remember hearing a colleague say, 'Well, I only have to do this job for another 15 years before I can retire.' He had both hope and resignation in his voice.'

Some people keep their own purpose quiet at work and then fulfil it in their personal life, e.g. by volunteering or becoming involved in a charity. This is a way of addressing a common dilemma for mismatching purposes.

The main issue is that we should look for a synergy between our personal purpose and that of the organisation. Then, if that is not possible, we need to learn to compromise in a good way and live with it. Organisations have a responsibility to live their purpose in an honest and ethical manner and create systems that reflect that.

E. Material resources and the environment

The final factor that is often forgotten and linked to purpose is that most of us partly depend on our material resources to gain a sense of well-being. This applies to both individuals and organisations. For those of us who are relatively comfortable, what do we think is vital? Often what we think of as non-negotiable and necessary would be a luxury for someone else. 'For example, every Friday, I order specialist desserts from my favourite patisserie. Are they necessary, no? Even though they are a part of my weekly stress management plan.'

We can determine how much we depend on material goods by carrying out a simple audit based on personal planning methods used in services for people with differences. Write all the material goods that help you maintain a sense of well-being and healthiness. Categorise them into those that are non-negotiable and vital, essential, and luxuries.

Now, stop and reflect. How many of the non-negotiables and essentials are exactly that? What could you let go of? What non-material strategy could you adopt instead? 'For example, instead of buying desserts every Friday, I could learn about breathing and mindfulness.'

You can also do this at an organisational level. What material goods do you have that are vital to the purpose and overall well-being and healthiness? A favourite to consider is the size of people's offices, that is often determined by seniority and not function. What is not needed or luxury or vital?

If an organisation is going to ensure the overall healthiness of all its staff, then it needs to ensure that people's basic needs are met, e.g. a decent wage with benefits. Ideally, there also needs to be more equality in terms of income across the board. 'I am still mystified why a nurse usually earns so much less than a film star. I guess it depends on how you judge worth in terms of work. Some will say that a film star has greater impact while others will argue that, in terms of meaningful work to help human beings, the nurse's work is more important.'

We have become complacent in terms of sustainability The climate crisis has almost been forgotten about except when there are global conferences such as COP26. What role does sustainability have in your world? To what extent is it sufficient? How much more is needed? It is worth exploring the UN Sustainable Development Goals and thinking about what more you could do.

F. Diversity

In Buddhism, there are the Ten Royal Rules for governance, and these are excellent to consider and see how you, either as a leader or organisation, can incorporate them so that all are looked after in terms of global healthiness. They include making sure those who are in need are looked after, being exemplary, upright, and straightforward; gentle yet impartial, having composure, being ready to forgive, to acknowledge and reward loyalty; to be and promote non-violence and be non-revengeful.

Each person, group, and culture will have its own perspective on overall healthiness. Some cultures will more easily focus on looking after the collective than the individual. We all need to respect our various perspectives a little more than we normally do. 'I was in Sri Lanka on 28th March 2005, when the second earthquake happened in Indonesia. I was staying in the northeast and was woken up at midnight by my colleague who told me it was highly likely that there would be another tsunami (like the one on 26th December 2004) and we needed to follow instructions and go to higher ground as our house was next to the beach. Mary and I had two cars and drivers prepared to take us to the office up the hill.

We saw everyone was awake around us. Mary said that we had spare spaces in the cars and would anyone like to join us. We were told politely that our neighbours preferred to remain with family and friends in case something happened. We left feeling a little guilty. Fortunately, there was not another massive tsunami as the tectonic plates had shifted horizontally and not vertically.'

It is worth taking time to explore your own approach to diversity and difference. We all have biases and perspectives, some of which we are unaware. Talking to those who are outside your normal social circle can be enlightening. The work of Fons Trompenaars is worth reading. Erin Meyer's book, *The Culture Map*, uses Fons Trompenaars's work and provides many examples of difference and diversity.

Including different voices

For there to be genuine compassion and overall health, we need to consider how we have included people with differences in our leadership and organisations. Having an inclusive survey or diversity expert or representative staff group is a start, but these interventions mean the messages are handed over and often interpreted or misinterpreted by those in power. A more inclusive approach, such as having someone with a difference at the table and whose voice is listened to for both small and large issues, is vital.

Maybe the person or a group need help to learn how to operate at that level and we should give this respectfully. 'The committee of a charity decided it needed to become more inclusive of its membership and have someone with differences as part of it. The person, who was selected by the wider membership, asked for and was given help in reading board papers ahead of time, could stop and ask questions for clarification in the meeting, and was supported by an external person in the meeting until they felt confident enough, e.g. understanding the jargon being used.'

When people's voices are heard, they may want to say much about their experience as they have felt silenced for so long. Taking the time to listen is part of the journey to inclusion. There are also methodological techniques that can be adopted, such as Asset Based Community Development (John McKnight). People with differences could also be invited to be part of groups that help solve problems: key actors could learn about the problem to be resolved and think about what they would like to say about the issue (either separately or collectively) and then come together to share and resolve the difficulty. This could become a regular practice.

Summary

What is desirable is an outcome achieved by living and working responsibly with balance between the four sources. And a clearer and changed sense of Self that will facilitate overall healthiness.

Please pause and think about yourself in this slightly different way. Consider what you have learned about yourself (individually or collectively) from the earlier exercises and then use the diagram below to write the actions and behaviours you will take to enhance your overall healthiness. Remember to think about and include linkages back to Self for each category.

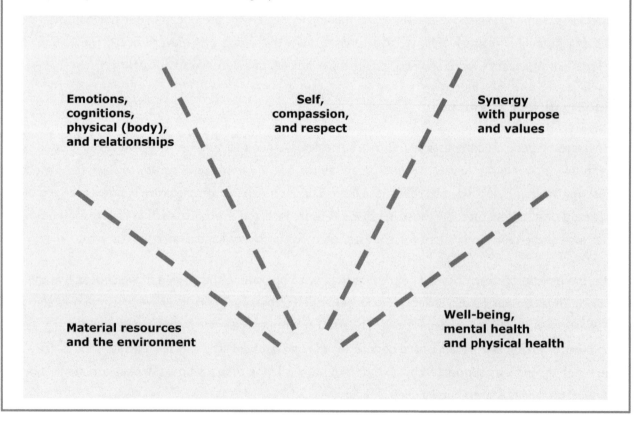

G. Living with the shadow side

Look back at the analyses that you have done as part of reading this book. What have you learned about your blend of golden and shadow? What does this say about your sense of Self?

The learning...

The shadow side can feel like an abyss that is scary to investigate. What have you learned about yours because of the earlier explorations? 'Mine is full of old memories, regrets, and wishing that I had done things differently. For example, sending an unnecessary email to a friend ten years ago and who, despite my apology, has yet to speak to me. And I can't blame her.'

Our shadow sides are very unlikely to disappear overnight. They can, however, decrease in effect and impact through constant reflection and practice. We suggest it is best to acknowledge their presence, address what we can comfortably, but know that it will take time to shift from the shadow side. A complete removal of the shadow side, experience tells us, is virtually impossible.

Sometimes it is useful to do some exercises, now and again, to help us look at what is in our shadow, and resolve where possible, so that the shadow becomes less powerful in our daily life. This can help to some extent and sometimes significantly decreases the impact of the memory or issue.

Of course, there may be some long-term effects of the shadow of which we are oblivious until we are ready to 'see' them. For example, suddenly realising you dislike a particular ice cream because it was the dessert you had at a very difficult and embarrassing official meeting years ago.

So, what can we do what to consider positively the shadow elements of our lives? As we have noted, an unwise approach would be to ignore it. It is important to find ways of acknowledging its presence in our lives and then look to see how it can be included helpfully.

Think back to what you have learned about the golden and shadow and the connectedness with your Self and other parts as an individual or an organisation. If you want to work on the shadow, how else could its function and purpose be met? How could you respond differently to the triggers? What is needed to maintain and enhance the golden?

The second step is, as you have done, to articulate the shadow aspects of words/thoughts, emotions, or behaviours. Then, ideally, with support, find ways of continuing to explore the shadow comfortably and consider (afterwards) what is the connection with the Self and how can the other components help? Here are some suggested approaches.

Find a quiet and comfortable place (perhaps with a trusted person), write or draw your shadow side. Sit with your outputs and let the emotions arise. Wait until they have dissipated, explore the purpose and function. Which parts of your golden side can help to counterbalance the shadow? Then think about which shadow behaviours you can replace with a positive aspect and which you could let go of. On a second piece of paper, write or draw the replacement behaviours and emotions. Stop and let yourself feel. Then, when you are ready, say goodbye and destroy securely the first piece of paper or art. Keep the remaining paper or art for the next time.

This is an exercise you can repeat as often as you want.

You could do a similar exercise in a large group. In a vast room, assign one wall for shadow aspects, one for golden aspects, and one for the Self. Gather key individuals and ask them to populate the walls using Post-its. They could start by describing each element in words or drawings. Then ask everyone to walk around the room and reflect on the outputs. Encourage them to think about how serious the shadow aspects are including their impact, what forgiveness is required and what needs to be let go of or replaced. Request the group also to reflect on what is golden and what is the Self.

Host a conversation about what overall healthiness means (perhaps use our definitions) for the group and then ask them to select what can stay, what needs to be replaced, and what needs to be removed. Encourage people to put their ideas down in three areas on the floor. Take away the pile of issues to be removed and ask people how they feel now and to commit to the new perspective.

You could also, as individuals or groups, imagine having a discussion with the shadow aspects and ask which ones need to stay or go. How can the golden help with the shadow side? What has happened to the Self? Then complete the conversation by asking people to make a note of their decisions.

You could, on a daily or weekly basis, spend some time on the extent to which you lived and worked from your golden side and/or the shadow side. What is your learning and how will you cope from now on?

Alternatively, you could use the diagram below to reflect on your week. In which quadrant did you live and work, mostly? What have you learned and what needs to be improved or let go of?

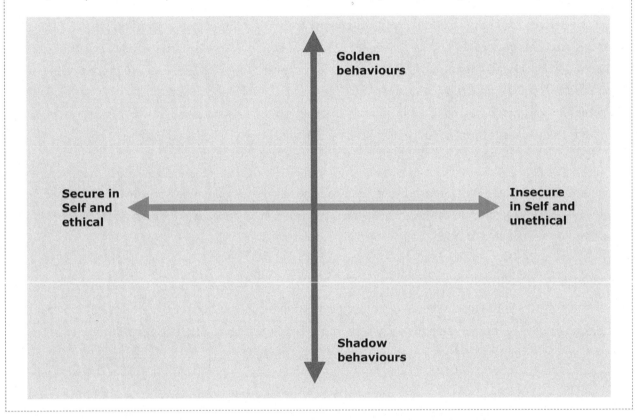

If you are someone or a group who has dwelled on the shadow side and are ready to shift to using more golden aspects of yourself, then please start with celebrating the golden. What is wonderful about you and your sense of Self? Then note down your shadow parts and think about what is needed to let go and move to the golden. Who and what will help you? What is the path you want to take?

Sometimes, large changes are too much. You could start with small steps such as not ignoring people, if that is one of your behaviours, to making sure you politely greet colleagues. Some people may not believe the change at first, but if you persist, they are likely to adjust their perspective of you.

Imagine a long line in a room from golden to shadow. Stand in the shadow part and look ahead to the golden. Imagine that you are being accompanied by your Self. Slowly start walking towards the golden part and imagine how you feel as you are moving towards the golden. Once you have arrived at the golden part, stop, and think about what/who could have helped you on your journey. What have you learned about your Self? This could become a weekly practice.

Dr Sousan Abadian has created, based on her research with healing indigenous communities, the ARIA (Awareness, Responsibility, Imagination, Action) framework which can explore the shadow side. It was originally derived for healing individual and community trauma. The first step is to notice self and the erroneous assumptions, beliefs, and narratives held. Second, the person or group is advised to consider the assumptions, beliefs, and narratives and re-write them or replace them so that they are more positive and aspirational. Third, it is time to become open once more to inspiration and the possibility of what the person or community wants to be and focus on that as opposed to the current perspectives. Finally, people are guided to use the aspirations to design next steps and act as though the desired future is here.

Think about your life and how much balance there is between the golden and shadow. How would you describe this? How constant is the balance? What is the function and purpose of the balance for you? What could you do to ensure a healthier and more constant balance?

With all the exercises above, there may be times when you regret what you did or said when in the shadow part of yourself. It is important to find ways of forgiving yourself (as needed) and, if possible, work out how to put things right. As human beings, we are all imperfect and fallible. The principal thing is to stop and reflect, learn, and return to the more positive aspects of yourself.

Occasionally, an individual or a group is not at all ready to let go of the shadow side. The Netflix series, *How to Fix a Drug Scandal*, provides an example. Two attorneys from the Attorney General's office in Massachusetts deliberately did not disclose vital information to defence attorneys in 2013. When asked in court, much later (2016), if they admitted to these omissions, one of them, Kris Foster still declined. Judge Richard J. Carey, who presided in 2016, called their actions 'a fraud upon the court' and underscored 'her lack of a moral compass'.

Here are some traps into which we can fall if we want to avoid changing and so stay on the shadow side: lying to yourself, ignoring your history and purpose, not dealing with using shadow behaviours such as lying or being jealous, and letting that affect your interactions. The fundamental way to address these traps requires honesty, integrity, compassion, respect, and courage. With these, we can avoid most of the traps.

If, for lesser shadow behaviours, this is not the right time for you to change, at the very least, please make sure that people are comfortable and respected. If you want to keep shadow behaviours and some traps, this could mean that you have built a closed and protective mindset with restricted critical thinking and behaving. Perhaps you could give yourself the permission to wonder what it would be like if you moved away from this mindset. What will help you feel secure in a more positive way?

Helping someone look at their shadow side requires certain approaches. First, it is important not to be judgemental, as we are all capable of living from the shadow side. The second aspect is to understand that the person may be frightened of acknowledging the negative impact that they have had. They may also fear realising the current influence of their past or unknown parts of themselves. If the person has asked for help, then it is important to first help them understand you are there to walk alongside them on the journey and support them as they want. Help them first to acknowledge their golden aspects and then explore the shadow side at a time and pace that is comfortable.

If, however, the person is not ready, then there is little to be done except let them know you are available if, and when, they want help. Perhaps suggest that, while they are pondering, they need to make sure that they and others will be OK.

Summary

> Here are some questions to consider.
>
> How will you live with and include your shadow side so that it does not adversely impact your Self?
>
> What is needed to obtain and maintain a greater balance between golden and shadow?
>
> What will you do if you, occasionally, operate from the shadow side?
>
> Therefore, what are the actions and practices that you will incorporate on a regular and sustained basis? How will you know you are maintaining them? When will you stop and reflect? Who can help you stick to your intentions?

H. Administrative issues

There may well be some administrative issues that need to be addressed. For example, reviewing the current HR policies to ensure that they promote golden and not shadow behaviours. If that is the case, then please make a note of them and work out a plan for change.

Another vital area is the existence of a trusted internal justice system such as a complaints procedure, the existence of an ombudsperson. You could think about introducing one or seeing what is needed to make the existing system more operational and trusted.

I. Leadership and organisational interventions

1. Currently available interventions

There are so many interventions to enhance individual and collective leadership and we are generally aware of them, e.g. coaching, mentoring, programmes. Most of them are usually helpful in building the golden side of ourselves. Similarly, there is a wide range of organisational interventions that can be used, e.g. strategies, change management, etc.

We recommend that, because humans and organisations are so very complex, you select a smorgasbord of interventions. Some may include traditional interventions such as coaching, education, leadership programmes or change management or re-structuring. What is vital is that whatever the interventions are, they must address both the golden and shadow aspects and lead (hopefully) to healthier leaders and organisations.

It is important to take time to make sure that you are open-minded when choosing so that you select what is needed instead of what you know and may be comfortable with. Think of the music world and the great songs and music that really go through to your core. The authors and creators of these songs and music let themselves be open to all possibilities, and were connected with their core, so that they created what was needed. We ought to be that open as we create solutions for healthier leadership and organisations.

For example, if you decide that you or someone else would benefit from coaching or a leadership programme, then please ensure that experienced people with the right expertise and qualifications offer these. The test of their proficiency will lie in how they use their knowledge and expertise and apply those to your situation. Coaching provided by an actor/coach can make a vast difference.

Alternatively, if you are thinking of a bigger intervention such as a leadership programme or a change management intervention, then please ensure that these include elements to change behaviour as well as concepts to think about. Having leadership programmes that include behavioural interventions is also much better than having traditional ones. Hugh Flanagan offered a programme that first identified the core problems in a healthcare organisation. Second, cohorts of key leaders were selected. They were placed in problem-solving groups and, simultaneously (through modules) introduced to leadership and organisational concepts that they then applied to address the problems.

2. Indices for healthy individuals and organisations

As suggested by Michael Emery, one of our experts, we have articulated some indices below to help identify where you are (as a leader or an organisation) and this may help you think about where you should focus your energies.

We suggest that there are four general overall health levels:

Platinum—an abundance of golden behaviours in many aspects of an individual or organisation and any minor shadow behaviours that arise are addressed, learned from, and converted to the golden. The golden is present and available 95% of the time or more. All roles depict and use mostly golden behaviours.

Gold—continuous balance between golden and shadow behaviours for a leader or the organisation. The balance shifts and changes occasionally, but the golden is present at least 75% of the time. Shadow behaviours exist but are generally not significant enough to negate the impact of the golden. The shadow is being addressed slowly but surely. Roles depict and use golden behaviours.

Silver—balance between golden and shadow but it is variable and not present over 50% of the time. Daily events and circumstances influence the presence and use of golden or shadow behaviours. There are some efforts to promote the golden, but very few to deal with the shadow side. Roles focus on the use of shadow behaviours with a few golden behaviours.

Bronze—preponderance of shadow behaviours and these are present 75% of the time or more, sometimes masquerading as golden behaviours. The shadow behaviours have been normalised and accepted. There are token attempts to promote golden behaviours, but it is recognised that these are not to be taken seriously. Negative behaviours are simply rewarded, tacitly and overtly. Roles encourage the use of shadow behaviours.

You could, either as an individual leader or organisation, work out where you are against these levels and then determine where you need to be. If you prefer this approach, we have provided some suggestions and actions for each level, in the appendix.

And finally, plans for change

A reality check

And here is an opportunity for you to make sure that your plans are realistic and that you are ready. We suggest that you use the diagram below to locate all your planned actions to make sure that you have made good choices. If not, then please consider changing them.

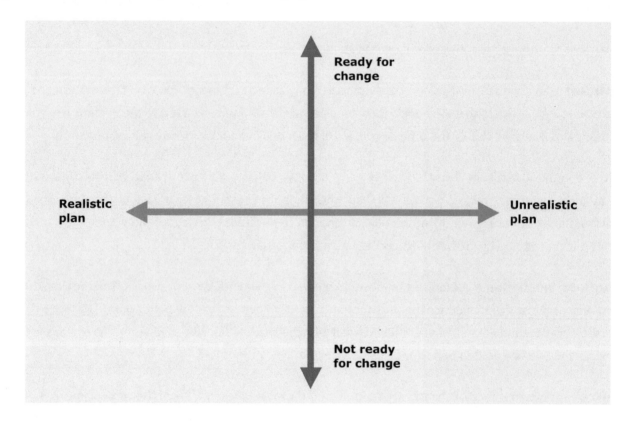

For individuals

Here are some steps to take to devise your own plan for change.

Looking at the key areas for overall healthiness, which interventions will you select?

What will you do to live with the shadow side?

What will be your renewed sense of Self? What type of leader do you want to be? What is the promise you will keep, either for yourself or the organisation or the wider world? What will be your role? What will be your likely impact?

Therefore, what will be the key elements of your plan and who will help you?

Area	Description	Timeframe/Helpers
Self, compassion, and respect		
Well-being, mental health, and physical health		
Emotions, cognitions, physical (body), and relationships		
Synergy with purpose and values		
Material resources and the environment		
Diversity		
Living with the shadow side		
Administrative issues		
Leadership and organisational interventions		
Anything else		

For organisations

Here are some steps to take to devise the plan for change.

Looking at the key areas for overall healthiness, which interventions will you select?

What will people in the organisation do to live with the shadow side?

What is the reframed sense of Organisational Self? What type of leadership and roles are needed? How will you attain these?

What type of followership is needed? How will it be encouraged?

What administrative matters need to be tackled?

Which type of organisation do you want to be? What will be your likely impact? What is the promise you will keep, for the organisation and the wider world?

Therefore, what will be the key elements of your plan and who will help you?

Area	Description	Timeframe/Helpers
Self, compassion, and respect		
Well-being, mental health, and physical health		
Emotions, cognitions, physical (body), and relationships		
Synergy with purpose and values		
Material resources and the environment		
Diversity		
Living with the shadow side		
Administrative issues		
Leadership and organisational interventions		
Anything else		

How do you feel at the end of this part of your journey?
Thank you and we wish you well.

Appendices

Appendix One: Indices For Healthy Leadership And Organisations

Michael Emery recommended we develop a Healthy Leadership Index, and that is a brilliant idea for which we are grateful.

Indices can be very helpful if they are not prescriptive. People and organisations are so very different and this needs to be recognised and reflected in an index. Similarly, we need a framework that provides some guidance. We used our models (Chapter One) as the basis for the Indices. The most important factor is the extent to which there is a balance or imbalance between the golden and shadow behaviours and the effect these have on individual leaders and organisations.

We have deliberately designed a qualitative method so that there is greater scope—flexibility that will, hopefully, lead to more creativity. We wanted something that reflected the complexity of humans when assessing Self and organisations.

Please use, change, or adapt our suggestions as you see fit. Once you have decided where you are in terms of the standards, you could return to Chapter Seven and decide what actions to take.

Here, once again, are our definitions of healthy leadership and health organisations.

What is overall healthiness?

The words healthy and healthiness usually refer to physical health and, sometimes, mental health and well-being. All these facets are important components for overall healthiness, but we suggest that there are others that also must be taken into consideration. These include the degree of synergy between purpose, values, and how life is lived and work conducted; the impact of material resources and the environment; being willing to be open and listen to the incoming future and finally how we live and cope with the shadow side.

All these factors, for overall healthiness, need to be coordinated with compassion and respect by our individual or organisational sense of Self.

What is healthy leadership?

Leadership is an individual and collective function that has many intentions. This usually includes an aim to serve human beings and/or something. For some, leadership is operationalised ethically and positively to serve others. Others will have another focus, such as a profit motive alongside wanting to be ethical.

Healthy leadership happens when the individual or the group do their utmost to serve others ethically and respectfully, while acknowledging that there can be negativity and being willing to address it and heal. They remain flexible and open to sensing the incoming future.

What is a healthy organisation?

Why do organisations exist? Usually, to enact a greater purpose which can be forgotten as the organisation becomes bigger and veers from the intended path.

A healthy organisation ensures it remains true to its purpose, and that is to do no harm to humans or the planet. Do no harm. The organisation always endeavours to provide a nourishing culture and structure within which people can grow and flourish in their work to achieve the purpose. A healthy organisation works to recognise and address unhealthy elements, is amenable to change and is willing to consider possible futures while operating in the present.

The overall health levels

Platinum—an abundance of golden behaviours in many aspects of an individual or organisation and any minor shadow behaviours that arise are addressed, learned from, and converted to the golden. The golden is present and available 95% of the time or more. All roles depict and use mostly golden behaviours.

Gold—constant and continuous balance between golden and shadow behaviours for a leader or the organisation. The balance shifts and changes on occasion, but the golden is present at least 75% of the time. Shadow behaviours exist but are generally not significant enough to negate the impact of the golden. The shadow is being addressed slowly but surely. Roles depict and use largely golden behaviours.

Silver—balance between golden and shadow but it is variable and not present over 50% of the time. The presence and use of golden or shadow behaviours is influenced by daily events and circumstances. There are some efforts to promote the golden, but very few to deal with the shadow side. Roles focus on the use of shadow behaviours with a few golden behaviours.

Bronze—preponderance of shadow behaviours and these are present 75% of the time or more, sometimes masquerading as golden behaviours. The shadow behaviours have been normalised and accepted. There are token attempts to promote golden behaviours, but it is recognised that these are not to be taken seriously. Negative behaviours are simply rewarded, tacitly and overtly. Roles generally encourage the use of shadow behaviours.

The judgement of what 95% or 25% means has been deliberately left open and as a qualitative decision. The table below provides some explanation.

Here are more detailed descriptions of the levels. If you choose to use this approach to judge yourself (individually or collectively), it is possible that there could some variability, e.g. platinum for some issues and silver for others. This is probably realistic and should be used as a stepping stone to the future.

INDEX FOR INDIVIDUAL LEADERS

OVERALL HEALTH LEVEL	PLATINUM	GOLD	SILVER	BRONZE
AREA/ ELEMENTS				
Sense of Self and coordination	Very positive, stable, and connected in harmony with all elements (see below).	Positive, stable, and connected well to some elements (see below).	Sometimes positive and stable, rarely connected to other elements (see below) or not positively.	Not positive, maybe stable and disconnected or connected but not positively.
Presence and use of golden and shadow behaviours	Golden>Shadow 95%.

The leader knows and understands all their behaviours and focusses very much on the golden side. | Golden>Shadow 75%.

The leader knows and understands most of their behaviours and focusses mostly on the golden side. | Golden=Shadow 50%.

The leader knows and understands (perhaps) their behaviours and uses mainly shadow behaviours. | Golden<Shadow 25%.

The leader accepts and only uses shadow behaviours. Their rationale can vary from being fine with their use to denying there is a problem. |

Culture, cognitions, emotions, physical (body), and relationships (including leadership)	Culture and relationships are overall golden and positive. Leaders and managers work together most of the time. All are treated with compassion and complete respect. Work practices, styles of thinking and decision making are positive and helpful to the overall purpose.	Culture and relationships are golden and positive. Leaders and managers work together some of the time. Most are treated with compassion and respect. Work practices, styles of thinking and decision making are sometimes positive and helpful to the overall purpose.	Culture and relationships are sometimes golden and positive. Leaders and managers rarely work together. Some are treated with compassion and respect. Work practices, styles of thinking and decision making are rarely positive and helpful to the overall purpose.	Culture and relationships are mainly shadow. Leaders and managers always in conflict or work from the shadow side. Very few (the favoured) are treated with compassion and respect. Work practices, styles of thinking and decision making are tailored to enhance the shadow side and the express purpose of a few.
Values, ethics, and purpose	Used actively as part of daily practice, both thinking and behaviours. The leader is clear about their sense of purpose, and this is shared and understood.	Used on most occasions. The leader is sometimes clear about their sense of purpose, and this is sometimes shared and understood.	Used sometimes. The leader is not clear about their sense of purpose, and this is not shared. Alternatively, their sense of purpose is self-serving to a large extent.	Rarely used. The leader's sense of purpose is not positive and not shared or is completely self-serving.

Well-being, mental health, and physical health	Takes excellent care of self and others.	Takes good care of self and others.	Takes limited care of self and others. Alternatively, largely looks after self and those deemed important.	Ignores personal health needs and those of others. Alternatively, only looks after self and those deemed important.
Interacting with the wider world and community	Meaningful interactions, incorporates sustainability fully.	Useful interactions, incorporates sustainability most of the time.	Spasmodic interactions sometimes include sustainability.	Ignores what is happening externally or misuses it.
Material resources and the environment	All resources are used wisely and sensibly.	Most resources are used sensibly.	There is a little sensible use of resources.	Resources are used for personal gain.
Where the person lives and works	Very conducive in promoting the golden.	Helpful in promoting the golden.	Not very helpful in promoting the golden.	Not at all helpful, promotes negativity.
Administrative	Ensures that all administrative matters, e.g. policies, procedures, strategies, reflect the golden and provide mechanisms to address the shadow side. These are operationalised fully.	Ensures that most administrative matters, e.g. policies, procedures, strategies, reflect the golden and provide mechanisms to address the shadow side. Most of these are operationalised fully.	Few administrative matters, e.g. policies, procedures, strategies, reflect the golden and provide mechanisms to address the shadow side. Few of these are operationalised fully.	Very little attention is paid to policies, procedures, and strategies except for promotion and maintenance of the shadow side
History	Personal history and its role is fully acknowledged and integrated with daily life.	Personal history and its role is generally acknowledged and integrated with daily life.	Personal history and its role is rarely acknowledged or integrated with daily life.	Personal history and its role is never accepted or acknowledged. Denial is very likely.
Anything else?				

INDEX FOR ORGANISATIONS

OVERALL HEALTH LEVEL	PLATINUM	GOLD	SILVER	BRONZE
AREA/ ELEMENTS				
Organisational sense of Self and roles	Very positive, compassionate, realistic, and respectful. Connected harmoniously with other elements.	Positive, compassionate, realistic, and respectful. Connected sometimes harmoniously with other elements.	Spasmodically positive, compassionate, and respectful. Occasionally in synchrony with other elements or not in a positive way.	Negative and disrespectful. Rarely connected to other elements or not positively.
Presence and use of golden and shadow behaviours	Golden>Shadow 95%. Nearly all understand and use golden behaviours and learn and change if shadow behaviours are used.	Golden>Shadow 75%. Most understand and use golden behaviours. They learn and sometimes change if shadow behaviours are used.	Golden=Shadow 50%. Very few understand and use golden behaviours and do not address the use of shadow behaviours.	Golden<Shadow 25%. Shadow behaviours are the norm, golden behaviours are rarely used or rewarded.
Formal and informal leadership	All leaders and managers work in tandem and democratically. Open consultation and communication.	Leaders and managers collaborate and work together most of the time with consultation and communication.	Leaders and managers sometime work together with some consultation and communication.	Very, very limited collaboration and cooperation. Leaders and managers often work against each other.

Cognitions, emotions, physical (body), and culture, work practices and relationships (including leadership)	The focus of both the culture and relationships is on healthiness including diversity.	The focus of both the culture and relationships is generally on healthiness including diversity.	The focus of both the culture and relationships is sometimes on healthiness including diversity.	The focus of both the culture and relationships is rarely on healthiness including diversity.
	All staff are treated with utmost respect.	Most staff are treated with a lot of respect.	Some staff are treated with respect.	Very few staff are treated with respect.
	Thinking, decision making, and work practices are helpful and effective.	Thinking, decision making, and work practices are sometimes helpful and effective.	Thinking, decision making, and work practices are rarely helpful and effective.	Thinking, decision making, and work practices are not helpful or effective except for a few.
	Any shadow behaviours that may arise are dealt with quickly.	Most shadow behaviours that may arise are dealt with.	Some shadow behaviours that may arise are dealt with.	Shadow behaviours are allowed and encouraged.
Values, ethics, and purpose	These are core, understood and lived by all.	These are central, understood and generally used.	These are known but only used sometimes.	These are ignored except when it is to someone's advantage.
Well-being, mental health, and physical health	The well-being, mental health, and physical health of all staff is paramount.	The well-being, mental health, and physical health of most staff is important.	The well-being, mental health, and physical health of some staff is considered.	The well-being, mental health and physical health of staff is not seen as important.
Interacting with the wider world and community	There is synergy with the wider world and sustainability for all is prime.	There is some synergy and connectedness with the wider world and community.	The wider world and community's presence is noted but not factored in significantly.	The needs of the wider world are ignored or used to the advantage of the organisation.

Legislation, policies, procedures, and organisational structures	All administrative elements are supportive of the aims of a healthy organisation. Where needed, they are fully implemented.	Most administrative elements are supportive of the aims of a healthy organisation. Where needed, they are generally implemented.	Some administrative elements are supportive of the aims of a healthy organisation. Where needed, they are sometimes implemented.	Very few administrative elements are supportive of the aims of a healthy organisation. Where needed, they are rarely implemented.
Material resources, where people work	Excellent care and thought have gone into this, and staff feel very comfortable. All adjustments for diverse needs are known and resourced.	A lot of care and thought has gone into this, and staff feel comfortable. Most adjustments for diverse needs are known and generally resourced.	Some care and thought have gone into this, and staff sometimes feel comfortable. Some adjustments for diverse needs are known and resourced.	Very limited care and thought have gone into this, and staff feel uncomfortable. Few adjustments for diverse needs are known and resourced.
Organisational history	History is honoured and learned from; anniversaries are celebrated.	History is noted and sometimes learned from and acknowledged.	History is generally ignored and not acknowledged.	Almost complete denial of the importance of history unless it reinforces the current toxic zeitgeist.
Anything else?				

Having considered these, you could (following discussions), complete the tables below. Remember that we have already discussed many of the interventions you could select in Chapter Seven.

ASSESSMENT AND PLAN FOR INDIVIDUALS

OVERALL HEALTH LEVEL AREA/ELEMENTS	MY CURRENT STATE	MY DESIRED STATE	ACTIONS
Sense of Self and coordination			
Presence and use of golden and shadow behaviours			

Cognitions, emotions, physical (body), culture, work practices and relationships (including leadership)			
Values, ethics, and purpose			
Well-being, mental health, and physical health			
Interacting with the wider world and community			
Material resources and the environment			
Where the person lives and works			
Administrative			
History			
Anything else?			

ASSESSMENT AND PLAN FOR ORGANISATIONS

OVERALL HEALTH LEVEL	MY CURRENT STATE	MY DESIRED STATE	ACTIONS
AREA/ELEMENTS			
Organisational sense of Self and roles			
Presence and use of golden and shadow behaviours			
Formal and informal leadership			
Cognitions, emotions, physical (body), and culture, work practices and relationships (including leadership)			
Values, ethics, and purpose			
Well-being, mental health, and physical health			
Interacting with the wider world and community			

Legislation, policies, procedures, and organisational structures			
Material resources, where people work			
Organisational history			
Anything else?			

Bibliography

Sousan Abadian. www.sousanabadian.com

Oana Albu and Mikkel Flyverbom (2016). Organizational transparency: conceptualizations, conditions, and consequences. DOI:10.1177/0007650316659851

American Psychological Association (2015). Stress in America survey. www.apa.org/topics/racism-bias-discrimination/types-stress www.apa.org/news/press/releases/stress/2015/impact

A

Dr. Eva Amundsdotter in Frida Jansson and Kristin Valasek (2021). How to guide: gender informed leadership. Folke Bernadotte Academy, Draft October 2021

Anti Corruption Resource Centre. www.u4.no/about-u4

Dan Ariely (2012). The (honest) truth about dishonesty. Harper Collins

Rebecca Ashton (2017). Professional courage: What does it mean for practitioner psychologists? Educational Psychology Research and Practice. Vol. 3, No. 1. Spring 2017. pp. 2–14

B	Simon Baddeley and Kim James (1987). Owl, fox, donkey or sheep: political skills for managers. DOI/10.1177/135050768701800101
	Greta Bauer (2021). Quantitative intersectional study design and primary data collection, Meet the Methods Series, Issue 3, part 1, February 2021. Institute of Gender and Health, Canadian Institute of Health Research
	Richard Beckhard (1997). Agent of change, my life, my practice. Jossey Bass.
	Tal Ben-Shahar. https://talbenshahar.com/
	Ås Berit (1978). Hersketeknikker. Kjerringråd. Vol.3, pp.17–21
	Robert Blake and Jane Mouton (1964). The managerial grid: key orientations for achieving production through people. Houston, Tex. Gulf Pub. Co.
	Chris Boeskool (2017). When you're accustomed to privilege, equality feels like oppression. (Huffpost, December 6, 2017)
	Danah Boyd. https://points.datasociety.net/agnotology-and-epistemological-fragmentation-56aa3c509c6b
	William Bridges. www.wmbridges.com
	British Standards Institute. https://www.bsigroup.com/en-GB/iso-45003/
	Burke, W.W. and Litwin G.H (1992). A causal model of organizational performance and change. https://DOI.org/10.1177/014920639201800306
C	www. Ckju.net
	Ciro Conversano, Alessandro Rotondo, Elena Lensi, Olivia Della Vista, Francesca Arpone,and Mario Antonio Reda (2010). Optimism and its impact on mental and physical well-being. DOI: 10.2174/1745017901006010025
	Kimberle Crenshaw (1989). Demarginalizing the intersection of race and sex: a black feminist critique of antidiscrimination doctrine, feminist theory and antiracist politics. University of Chicago Legal Forum, Vol 1989, issue 1
	Catalina Crespo-Sancho (2017). The role of gender in the prevention of violent conflict. Background paper for the United Nations-World Bank flagship study, Pathways for peace: inclusive approaches to preventing violent conflict. World Bank.
	Jo Cutler and Daniel Campbell-Meiklejohn (2018). Comparative fMRI meta-analysis of altruistic and strategic decisions to give. DOI: 10.1016/j.neuroimage.2018.09.009.

D	Antonio Damasio (2000). The feeling of what happens: body and emotion in the making of consciousness. Mariner Books

Jim Detert (2021). Choosing courage: the everyday guide to being brave at work. Harvard Business Review Press.

Martine Dove (2020). The psychology of fraud, persuasion and scam techniques.Routledge

Sylvia Duckworth (2021). Wheel of power/privilege. Institute of Gender and Health, Canadian Institute of Health Research.

Charles Duhigg (2012). The power of habit: why we do what we do in life and business. New York: Random House

Jane E. Dutton, Kristina M. Workman and Ashley E. Hardin (2014). Compassion at work. Annu. Rev. Organ. Psychol. Organ. Behav. Vol 1, pp. 277–304

Elizabeth Dunn and Laura Aknin (2008). Spending money on others promotes happiness. DOI:10.1126/science.1150952

DSM 5. Diagnostic and Statistical Manual 5. https://www.psychiatry.org/psychiatrists/practice/dsm |
| **E** | Amy C Edmondson and Mark Mortenson (2021) What psychological safety looks like in a hybrid workplace. https://hbr.org/2021/04/what-psychological-safety-looks-like-in-a-hybrid-workplace

Gerard Egan (1994). Working shadow side management: a guide to positive behind-the-scenes management. Jossey-Bass Management |
| **G** | www.gallup.com

Gerlach, P., Teodorescu, K. and Hertwig, R. (2019). The truth about lies: A meta-analysis on dishonest behavior. DOI:10.1037/bul0000174

Mura Ghosh (2020) https://london.ac.uk/senate-house-library/blog/PsychologyofKindness

Marc Gold. www. marcgold.com

https://www.goodreads.com/quotes/9133570

www.goodtherapy.org

UK Government. www.gov.uk/workplace-bullying-and-harassment

Martin Gold (Editor) (1999). The complete social scientist: a Kurt Lewin reader. American Psychological Association

Daniel Goleman (2020). Emotional intelligence: 25th anniversary edition. Bloomsbury Publishing |

H	Jonathan Haidt (2016). The Center for Compassion and Altruism Research and Education. http://ccare.stanford.edu/ Robert Hare (1999). Predators: The disturbing world or the psychopaths among us. Guilford Press Homayoun Hatami and Liz Hilton Segel (2021). https://www.mckinsey.com/business-functions/strategy-and-corporate-finance/our-insights/what-matters-most-five-priorities-for-ceos-in-the-next-normal Margaret Heffernan. www.mheffernan.com www.helpguide.org Hitsville: the making of Motown (2019). Directed by Ben Turner, Gabe Turner. Polygram Entertainment, Capitol Records and Motown Shae Hong. www.thriveglobal.com. The importance of honesty at work. How to fix a drug scandal (2020). Netflix. Director. Erin Lee Carr
I	I am not an easy man (2018). Netflix.Director. Éléonore Pourriat https://www.insurancequotes.com/business/revenge-in-the-workplace
J	Phil Jackson (2015). Eleven rings. Virgin Kim James and Tanya Arroba (2005). Reading and carrying: a framework for learning about emotion and emotionality in organisational systems as a core aspect of leadership development: Management Learning, Vol. 36 (3), pp. 299-316 Robert A Johnson (1993). Owning your own shadow, understanding the dark side of the psyche. Harper Collins. Abraham Juneman, Julia Suleeman and Bagus Takwin (2018). Psychological mechanism of corruption: a comprehensive review. Asian Journal of Scientific Research, Vol. 11, pp. 587-604. Carl Gustav Jung (1991). The archetypes and the collective unconscious (Collected Works of C. G. Jung). Routledge

K	Anita E. Kelley. A life without lies: how living honestly can affect health. Session 3189, 12 to 12:50 p.m., Saturday, Aug. 4, Room W303C, Level III, Orange County Convention Center. Dacher Keltner (2012). https://greatergood.berkeley.edu/article/item/the_compassionate_species Georgia Kenyon. https://www.bbc.com/future/article/20160105-the-man-who-st udies-the-spread-of-ignorance King's Fund. www.kingsfund.org.uk Kevin Kniffin and David Sloan Wilson (2004). The effect of nonphysical traits on the perception of physical attractiveness: Three naturalistic studies. Evolution and Human Behavior. Vol. 25(2), pp.88-101 Elisabeth Kubler-Ross and David Kessler (2014) On grief and grieving: finding the meaning of grief through the five stages of loss. Simon and Schuster
L	Danielle LaGree, Brian Houston, Margaret Duffy and Haejung Shin (2021). The effect of respect: respectful communication at work drives resiliency, engagement, and job satisfaction among early career employees. https://DOI.org/10.1177/23294884211016529 Richard Layard with George Ward (2020). Can We Be Happier? Evidence and Ethics. Pelican Leadership IQ Survey https://www.leadershipiq.com/blogs/leadershipiq/employee-engagement-is-les s-dependent-on-managers-than-you-think Heather S. Lonczak (2021). https://positivepsychology.com/why-is-compassion-important/ Rocío Lorenzo, Nicole Voigt, Miki Tsusaka, Matt Krentz, and Katie Abouzahr (2018). Diverse leadership teams boost innovation. Boston Consulting Group Losada https://www.worktolive.info/blog/bid/336460/how-optimism-boosts-productivity-and-work-life -balance Herb Lovett. Personal communication with Anna Eliatamby Lyman B., Gunn M. M., Mendon C. R. (2020). New graduate registered nurses' experiences with psychological safety. J. Nurs. Manage. 28 831–839. 10.1111/jonm.13006

M	A Maulidi (2020). When and why (honest) people commit fraudulent behaviours? Journal of Financial Crime. ISSN 1359-0790
	www.mayoclinic.org
	Peggy McIntosh (1989). White privilege: unpacking the invisible knapsack. Peace and Freedom. July/August 1989
	John McKnight. https://johnmcknight.org/
	www.mentalhealth.org.uk
	Erin Meyer (2016). The culture map: decoding how people think, lead, and get things done across cultures. Public Affairs
	Herman Miller (2012). The psychology of collaboration space. www.workplaceunlimited.com
	www.mindtools.com
	www.mind.org.uk
	Celia Moore (2015) Moral Disengagement. Current Opinion in Psychology. Vol. 6. pp. 199-204
	Mark Murphy (2020). https://www.forbes.com/sites/markmurphy/2020/02/26/optimistic-employees-are-103-more-inspired-to-give-their-best-effort-at-work-new-data-reveals/?sh=731e05e67afc
N	Tsedal Neeley (2021). mckinsey-on-books/author-talks-tsedal-neeley-on-why-remote-work-is-here-to-stay-and-how-to-get-it-right
	Ingjald Nissen (1945). Psykopatenes diktatur. H. Aschehoug
	Nitin Noria (2016). https://www.hbs.edu/about/leadership/dean/Pages/message-details.aspx?num=10571
O	David Owen and Jonathan Davidson (2009). Hubris syndrome: An acquired personality disorder? a study of US presidents and UK prime ministers over the last 100 year. Brain 2009: Vol. 132, pp. 1396–1406
	David Olusoga (2016). Black and British: a forgotten history. Picador

| P | Christopher Peterson and Martin Seligman (2004). Character strengths and virtues: A handbook and classification volume. Oxford University Press

Johnny Pitts (2019) Afropean: notes from Black Europe. Penguin UK

Ioana Pop (2016). And justice for all: Examining corruption as a contextual source of mental illness. DOI 10.1016/j.socscimed.2016.11.033

www.positivepsychology.com

Alvin Poussaint and James P. Come (1992). Raising Black Children, (originally titled Black Child Care (1975)). Plume: New York

James Prochaska and Carlo DiClemente (2005). The transtheoretical approach. In John C. Norcross and Marvin R. Goldfried (eds.). Handbook of psychotherapy integration. Oxford series in clinical psychology (2nd ed.). Oxford; New York: Oxford University Press. pp. 147–171

Robert N. Proctor (1995). The cancer wars: how politics shapes what we know and don't know about cancer. Basic Books. Also reported in https://www.bbc.com/future/article/20160105-the-man-who-studies-the-spread-of-ignorance

https://www.psychologytoday.com/gb

https://psychology.wikia.org/wiki/Psychology_Wiki |
|---|---|
| R | David Rand (2016). Cooperation, fast and slow. http://DOI.org/10.1177/0956797616654455

Christopher R Rate, Jennifer A Clarke, Douglas R Lindsay and Robert Sternberg (2007). Implicit theories of courage. DOI:10.1080/17439760701228755

Dennis Relojo-Howell (2021). Underperformance is often environmental. Psychreg.org

Chitra Reddy. https://content.wisestep.com/stop-fraud-corruption-workplace-best-tips/

www.resilientneighbourhoods.ca

Patsy Rodenburg (2009). Presence: how to use positive energy for success in every situation. Penguin. |

S	Eugene Sadler-Smith, Vita Akstinaite, Graham Robinson and Tim Wray (2016). Hubristic leadership: A review. https://DOI.org/10.1177/1742715016680666
	https://www.scb.se/hitta-statistik/artiklar/2016/Hog-utbildning-gar-i-arv/
	Martin Seligman.www.positivepsychology.com
	Anil Seth (2021). Being you: A new science of consciousness. Faber and Faber.
	Scarman Report on the 1981 Brixton riots; part 2. HOME AFFAIRS. Civil disorder: National Archives. Kew
	Richard Schwarz. https://www.psychotherapynetworker.org/magazine/article/2/facing-our-dark-side
	Mark Solms (2021). The hidden spring: a journey to the source of consciousness. Profile Books
	Statistics Sweden. https://www.scb.se/hitta-statistik/artiklar/2016/Hog-utbildning-gar-i-arv/
	Strengths Audit: www.strengthsprofile.com
	Makato Suzuki. https://www.youtube.com/watch?v=FCgwTSz4-_4&ab_channel=TEDxTalks
	Paul Slovic. https://www.bbc.com/future/article/20200630-what-makes-people-stop-caring
	Otto Scharmer. www.ottoscharmer.com
	Smriti Sharma, Saurabh Singhal, Saurabh, Finn Tarp (2021). Corruption and mental health: evidence from Vietnam. https://DOI.org/10.1016/j.jebo.2021.02.008
	Derald Wing Sue and Lisa Spanierman (2020). Microaggressions in everyday life. Wiley
T	J.R. Thorpe (2019). www.bustle.com
	Dennis Tourish (2018). Dysfunctional leadership in corporations. In Peter Garrard (Editor). The leadership hubris epidemic; Biological Roots and Strategies for Prevention. Palgrave
	Dennis Tourish (2020). Towards an organisational theory of hubris: symptoms, behaviours and social fields within finance and banking. Organization, Vol. 27(1) 88–109
	The last dance (2020). Director Jason Hehir. ESPN/Netflix
	Fons Trompenaars https://www2.thtconsulting.com/
U	UK Government. https://www.gov.uk/workplace-bullying-and-harassment

V	Carolina Valencia (2021). How to get employees to (actually) participate in wellbeing programs. https://hbr.org/2021/10/how-to-get-employees-to-actually-participate-in-well-being-programs Sophie Van Der Zee, Ross Anderson, and Ronald Poppe (2016). When lying feels the right thing to do. https://DOI.org/10.3389/fpsyg.2016.00734 www.verywellmind.com www.vogue.co.uk/arts-and-lifestyle/gallery/kamala-harris-best-quotes
W	B Allan Wallace. www.alanwallace.com Joseph T Wells (1997) Occupational fraud and abuse. Obsidian Publishing Co. David Wolfe and Dana R. Hermanson (2004). The fraud diamond: considering the four elements of fraud. CPA Journal, Vol 74(12), pp. 38-42 Monica Worline and Jane Dutton (2017). Awakening compassion at work: the quiet power that elevates people and organizations. Berrett-Koehler
Y	Jamie Yan (2019). www.simpplr.com/blog/2019/importance-of-collaboration-in-the-workplace/

Printed in Great Britain
by Amazon